Columbus Chronicles

Celebrating 200 Years of Columbus County, North Carolina

And Her People, 1808 – 2008

Volume 1, Number 1
December 2008

A Bicentennial Project of the

Southeastern North Carolina Genealogical Society

Edited by Alice Soles

Columbus Chronicles: Celebrating 200 Years of Columbus County, North Carolina and Her People, 1808 – 2008, *Vol. 1, No. 1, December 2008.*

Copyright © 2008 by the Southeastern North Carolina Genealogical Society

Published by the Southeastern North Carolina Genealogical Society (SENCGS), P. O. Box 463, Lake Waccamaw, N.C. 28450. All materials were provided by various contributors who are solely responsible for the content. All rights reserved.

Additional copies may be ordered at http://www.lulu.com/SENCGS.

Forward all corrections and material for submission in future issues to Alice Soles, editor, at CCLibrary@gmail.com. Submissions are preferred in digital format.

Cataloging Data*

    Columbus chronicles : celebrating 200 years of Columbus County, North Carolina and her people, 1808 – 2008, vol. 1, no. 1, December 2008 / edited by Alice Soles for the Southeastern North Carolina Genealogical Society. Lake Waccamaw, N.C. : Southeastern North Carolina Genealogical Society, 2008.

    63 p. : ill. 8 ½" x 11", paperback
Includes index.

    Library of Congress Control Number: 2008936387

    ISBN 978-0-615-24889-9

    1. Columbus County (N.C.) – History. 2. Columbus County (N.C.) – Genealogy.
       I. Southeastern North Carolina Genealogical Society. II. Soles, Alice III. Soles, Alice Jane Holmes.

    975'.631

Starting in January, SENCGS meets every other month at 2:00 PM at the North Carolina Museum of Forestry in Whiteville, North Carolina. Membership dues are $20.00 per year which includes six newsletters, but does not include these journals. Send dues to SENCGS, P. O. Box 463, Lake Waccamaw, NC 28450.

* *Cataloging data created by the editor.*

A Word from the President

One of the purposes of the Southeastern North Carolina Genealogical Society (SENCGS) is to preserve our history. That was the purpose for publishing *Columbus County, North Carolina Heritage 1808-2004*. We considered a second volume, but decided to publish a journal instead. Since Columbus County is observing its bicentennial, SENCGS is proud to publish the first issue of *Columbus Chronicles*, our contribution to the Columbus County Bicentennial observance.

We sought contributions from SENCGS members, as well as others, and were overwhelmed by the response. Not being able to use all of the material received in this first issue, further issues are assured. Please continue to submit your articles on the history, genealogy, stories, and tales regarding Columbus County, her people, and relations to the editor at CCLibrary@gmail.com for inclusion in subsequent issues.

SENCGS were saddened recently by the death of two of our most active members, Earl Williamson and Catherine Yates. For many years they were active in genealogy and the preservation of our history. They will be sorely missed. So with great pride we dedicate this first issue of *Columbus Chronicles* to Earl Williamson and Catherine Yates.

-- **Slade Skipper**

Farmer's Day Parade, Whiteville, 1951

On Madison Street in Front of the Columbus Theatre: Farmer's Day Queen.

Submitted by Pat Norris

TABLE OF CONTENTS

COLUMBUS COUNTY NORTH CAROLINA

A Word from the President 3
   Farmer's Day Parade, Whiteville, 1951 3
TABLE OF CONTENTS 4
ACME FERTILIZING COMPANY 5
   Background and History 5
   The Business Established 6
   Acme Fertilizer Company's Lasting Effect 6
   The Fertilizer Industry in Southeastern North Carolina 7
   Former Employees of Acme Fertilizer Co. 8
FAMILY MATTERS 10
   Shadrach Wooten and his Descendants ... 10
   Miller Family Migration to Bogue Twp. ... 12
   From Times Past: Miss Julie 14
Margaret Brown Wilson 15
   Mama's Story 15
   Mama's Mind Exercises 21
   The Year After 22
   Mama Said: 23
   "Let Me Get A Sack" 24
   Miz' Sally's Automobile 25
   Miss Sallie Brown and Mr. Obe Young ... 26
   A Grapevine, Collards & Stack of Wood 27
Irene Brown Shaw 28
   Sunday School Remembrances 28
   My Experience as a Teacher 28
   Redbug North Carolina Remembrances . 30
   Old Evergreen, NC 31
      An Oral Reminisce 31
      Evergreen Churches 31
      The Wonderful Big Oak of Evergreen 32
      An Evergreen Story Remembered 32
   1952 Evergreen Baseball Team 32
   Vance Fields' Story 33
   Wm Byron Pension 34

TALES OF COLUMBUS 35
   Preacher Crance Hardee 35
   Harvey Powell 35
   A Miracle for Cousin Kit 36
   Maxine Wright Mumaw 36
   Calvin Soles 37
   Joshua Long 37
   William Stedman Porter 37
   Susie Long Boswell 37
   Armegy R. Soles 38
   Beth Bruton 38
   Hance Wright 38
   Alfred S. Fowler 39
   The Stingiest Man in Mollie 39
   "The Picture Man" 40
   Skipper Compound Doesn't Work 40
   Russell Z. Bailey, Union Soldier 40
   The Wood Box 40
   The Junkman Comes on a Tuesday 41
HISTORICAL PERSPECTIVES 43
   Mill Branch Primitive Baptist Church 43
   The Charleston Earthquake of 1886 44
   Toys and Games 45
   Cemetery "Workings" & Other Musings 46
      Chadbourn Berry Growers 47
   Corrections to *Columbus County, North Carolina Heritage 1808-2004* 51
   Query 51
   Another Serving: Our Next Issue 51
IN MEMORIUM 52
   Catherine Simmons Yates 52
   Earl Williamson 53
      A Biography of Lenworth Earl Williamson ... 53
      Mama's Cow – The Golden Guernsey 55
      Memories of Earl Williamson 57
Index 59

ACME FERTILIZING COMPANY

ACME FERTILIZER COMPANY PLANT AT ACME, NORTH CAROLINA

Submitted by: Ernestine Keaton, writer historian, Riegelwood, NC.
Research by C. Bryant

Background and History

The Acme area was first settled in 1726 and was called Beaver Dam and was a part of an original land grant called Black Rock. The grant was given to Nathaniel Moore who along with other family members settled the Brunswick County town of Southport. The first settlement in this area of Columbus County was Grange Farm or Lloyd Landing, located off Hwy 11, along the Cape Fear, at the mouth of Weyman Creek. The surrounding area was, as far as we know, unpopulated pine forest.

At the beginning of the 1880s, the future town of Acme (then called Livingston) was little more than an oak ridge situated on the eastern bank of Livingston Creek. But that would change due to the efforts of Michael Cronly and Wilkes Morris. They were local carpetbaggers, members of a group of Wilmington investors and speculators who had invested in the Wilmington, Charlotte, and Rutherford Railroad. The areas along a sixty-mile stretch westward through the Piney Woods of Columbus County and Bladen County were scouted for possible business ventures.

The investment team of Cronly and Morris set their sights on the Acme area because of its location and the business activity that was already taking place there. All of the old plantations boat landings, including J. P. Robeson's at Livingston Creek were daily stops for cargo and passenger steamers traveling between Wilmington and Fayetteville. And less than a mile away Lloyd Landing was a bustling business center where large turpentine distillers and gristmills were available for use by large and small businesses from both sides of the Cape Fear. Not to be overlooked, there was another reason for investors to favor the area - the convenience of a new railroad system.

The completion of the Wilmington, Charlotte, and Rutherfordton Railroad (Carolina Central) in the mid 1870s, and the Atlantic Coast Line in the early 1900s, provided an additional, and more reliable mode of transporting goods to markets in Wilmington, and points beyond These developments were crucial to the growth of industry in Acme In addition to being one of the incorporators of the W.C.R.R.R, Mr. Cronly was one of the investors in the Navassa Guano Company, the first successful fertilizer factory in the Cape Fear Region.

December 2008 5

The Business Established

In 1883, Michael Cronly and Wilkes Morris partnered with William Lattimore to establish the first business on Livingston Creek, the Cronly Manufacturing Company which was a pine-oil refinery and a fibre mill. A few years later both businesses were destroyed by fire. In 1887 the first fertilizer factory was built, but it too was destroyed by fire. Subsequently, in the early 1890s, there was a larger factory in place and with former Cronly Fertilizer agents, G. Herbert Smith and William Gilchrist, as the new owners.

William Gilchrist

The new fertilizer company was named Acme, and because the name suggested quality and excellence, they put great effort into testing and mixing a high-grade fertilizer.

By the end of the century Acme Fertilizer was contributing to the production of seventy thousand tons of fertilizer a year, which was marketed in five states.

In 1905, Acme Fertilizer Manufacturing Company, being the chief industry in the village, owners of the village and the post office, petitioned to have the name of the village changed to Acme. Their petition was successful, and in 1911, the town of Acme was incorporated.

For several years, Gilchrist and Smith operated the fertilizer factory themselves, but around 1908, they hired B.S. Reynolds from Phoenix in Brunswick County, as the company superintendent. According to Bernard Troy, his grandfather, John Troy came to Acme Manufacturing Company with Reynolds. There is a strong possibility that Mr. Reynolds and Mr. Troy were previously employed by the Navassa fertilizer factory and, were hired for their experience in the fertilizer industry.

In the early 1920s, William Gilchrist bought out G. Herbert Smith. Towards the end of the decade, the increase in the number of black farmers, and in a subsequent higher demand for Acme fertilizer, prompted several changes at Acme Manufacturing Company. Under Mr. Gilchrist, the factory was enlarged, and more workers were hired. More importantly, the plant which had been operated by steam was converted to electricity.

It was common in those times for a company to include housing with employment. According to some former residents, Acme Fertilizer Company provided close to fifty four-room houses to accommodate the families of the fertilizer workers. There was also a company owned store near the housing area where the residents, as well as those living in the surrounding communities did their shopping.

By the early 1930s, Acme Fertilizer Company was headed by Thomas Wright I, a son-in-law of William Gilchrist. Wright steered the company through the Depression, or as some folks like to call it "Hoover Days". Times were tough, and money was tight, but work was still available at Acme Fertilizer.

Thomas Wright I

From the 1930s, to the 1960s, the labor force at Acme Fertilizer was mostly black farmers who worked during the winter months, or shipping season and used the spring lay-off to plant their own crops. The partnership between Acme Fertilizer and the seasonal worker who also brought fertilizer was beneficial to both parties.

Acme Fertilizer Company's Lasting Effect

In the late 1960s, after more than eighty years in existence, the Acme Fertilizer factory was torn down. It was the end of an era whereby Acme Fertilizer was a major source of revenue for Columbus County. More importantly, Acme Fertilizer had been a source of income for those who needed it the most - the black families who lived in the Acme area.

Today, most of the men who were there during the early years of Acme Fertilizer Company are no longer with us. But, there are men, such as Mr. Archie 'White' Brown, Mr. Edison Burns and Mr. Roger Waddell who can speak for, and about those workers from Armour, Northwest, Delco, Freeman, Bolton, and East Arcadia. The work ethic of that past generations of men at Acme Fertilizer Company set the standards for future generations of industry workers in rural Columbus County.

Willie Waddell – The Unofficial CEO. Many knew if they wanted a job, they had to see Mr. Waddell.

The Fertilizer Industry in Southeastern North Carolina

The fertilizer industry was created during the period of Reconstruction (the period following the Civil War) by a group of Wilmington lumber and railroad investors. The lumber industry, which had been shipping lumber to the West Indies since colonial days, began to express their concern over the luck of a profitable return crop. A group of investors came up with the idea that if the lumber ships were returned to the Cape Fear with cargoes of guano (bird droppings), a fertilizer industry might be established in the area. In 1867, R.R Bridges of the Wilmington-Weldon R.R, W.J. Hawkins of the Raleigh and Gaston R.R., and Edward Kidder, an importer of lumber, founded the Cape Fear Guano Company. The enterprise was a failure because the Carolina cotton farmers could not afford to buy the fertilizer. But two years later, those same investors, with others started the Navassa Guano Company. They were joined by the wealthy McCrae family who had already started a small-scale production of *Land Plaster9*, a fertilizer made from crude gypsum that was imported from Nova Scotia. Although the afore-mentioned men greatly influenced the growth of the fertilizer industry, it was the efforts of another individual whose ideas concerning the fertilizer industry was revolutionary.

George Zadoc French, was the flesh and blood historical reality of the hated carpetbagger, the group that some claimed ruled the Cape Fear counties of the Eighth District during Reconstruction. French held the distinction of being a New England Yankee, young, sharp-witted and brash, who during the war had engaged in the dubious occupation of an Army sutler. He was known to have conducted business with down and out returning union-prisoners by offering them loans and collecting 'IOUs'.

Of all French's various business dealings none evoked as much enthusiasm as the plantation he bought at Rocky Point, and named Excelsior. Instead of trying to play gentlemen and imitating the gentry, this hustling young man was brash enough to presume to teach lessons on farming to his neighbors- men whose families had been supervising plantations along the river for more than a century.

While neighboring planters stood by and watched their rice fields become primeval swamps, George French's Excelsior plantation was humming with activity. The reason was that George French believed in fertilizer. According to some, he took his beliefs to such extremes, they found it offensive.

During the evening hours when the people of Wilmington like to sit on their verandas and enjoy the cool breezes, the insufferable Yankee would have his sewage carts on the streets collecting harvests of 'fertilizer' that the citizens of Wilmington contributed to the fields at Excelsior. While everyone's thoughts were on retiring, French was "dragging his smelly loads through our public streets."

George French's zeal for fertilizer eventually led him to a source of supply that was more accessible than Wilmington night soil. He discovered limestone deposits at Excelsior, where he opened quarries and began manufacturing lime. He soon increased the number of workers to meet the demands from the local market. Overall, French pioneered an industry that would figure in the economy of the Cape Fear region in the twentieth century.

In the summer of 1872, French produced the first green ear of corn of the season to appear in the Cape Fear region. This was an important achievement because he had launched another industry, truck farming that would help revitalize the economy by producing early fruits and vegetables for sale to northern markets. But most importantly, he created a new class of farmers-- those who understood the benefits of fertilizer.

The success of the Navassa Guano Company could be attributed to the company's location and accessibility to the busy port city of Wilmington. Many would have considered it unlikely, that industry would also take hold more than thirty miles up the Cape Fear, in rural Columbus County.

But in 1883, the fertilizer industry was established in the village of Acme.

Former Employees of Acme Fertilizer Company

Ambert, John
Andrews, Charles
Andrews, Ed
Andrews, Herbert
Andrews, John
Andrews, McKinley
Ballard, Capot
Ballard, Charles
Ballard, Harlee
Ballard, Henry H.
Ballard, Van
Bellamy, Alex
Bibbs, Lemuel
Blake, Beaulah
Blake, Clay
Blizzard, Charles
Blizzard, George
Blizzard, Houston
Bowens, Benjamin
Bowens, Cliney
Bowens, Mack
Bowens, Raymond
Bowens, Tommy
Bowens, Willie
Bradley, Lewis
Bress, James 'Doc'
Bress, Sude
Bress, Will 'Sude'
Brown, Alfred
Brown, Archie "White"
Brown, Collis
Brown, Elijah
Brown, Emmitt
Brown, Hezekiah
Brown, J. B.
Brown, J. D.
Brown, James
Brown, Joe
Brown, John William
Brown, Leroy
Brown, McMurray
Brown, Oree
Brown, Randolph
Brown, Raymond 'Dock'
Brown, Sherwood
Brown, Steve

Brown, Willie
Bryant, Claddy
Bryant, David "Billy"
Bryant, Fred D.
Bryant, Freddy
Bryant, Gus
Bryant, Harry
Bryant, James
Bryant, James 'Buck'
Bryant, John
Bryant, Johnny
Bryant, Moss
Bryant, Richard
Bryant, Willie
Bullock, James
Burney, Roland
Burns, Al
Burns, Robb
Burns, Thomas Edison
Butler, Ruth
Butler, William 'Bill'
Carroll, Corbett
Carroll, Rodney
Carter, Abram
Carter, Alex
Champion, Joe
Clay, Earl
Clay, Fred
Cole, Arthur
Collins, Bud
Collins, Kiah
Compton, Clyde
Congleton, Donald
Congleton, Duf
Congleton, Duff
Congleton, Mose
Cook, Daniel
Corbett, Odell
Corbett, William
Covinghouse, Bill
Curtis, Bobby
Daniels, Clayton
Daniels, James E.
Daniels, James Eddie
Daniels, Theodore
Davis, Willie

Dew, Roy
Dixon, Cornelia
Dubar, Silas Jr.
Dubar, Silas Sr.
Eagle, James
Ellison, Sonny
Everett, Tony
Fields, Clarence
Fields, Willie
Flynn, Floyd
Folger, Archie
Folger, Madison
Formey, Noah
Formey, Prossie
Formey, Solomon
Formy Duval, Charles
Formy Duval, Charles C.
Formy Duval, Wilbur
Freeman, Charlie
Freeman, Robert 'Dick'
Freeman, Wesley
Freeman, Wesley
Gainey, Ted
Graham, Biney S.
Graham, Collis
Graham, Daniel "Dick"
Graham, Leon 'Hot Rod'
Graham, Phil
Grange, George
Gross, Frank Joseph, Sr.
Hall, Nathan
Hall, Richard
Hawkins, Stagie
Hickman, William "Bill"
Hill, Fletcher
Hobbs, John
Hudson, Garrett 'Ben'
Jackson, Bill
Jackson, Dave
Jackson, Fred
Jackson, McDuffie
Jones, Ben
Jones, Willie
Justice, Weldon
Keaton, Rufus
Keaton, Willie 'Buck'

Former Employees of Acme Fertilizer Company, cont.

Kellon, Vance
Kelly, Sam
King, John
Lacewell, Ed
Lloyd, Dave
Lloyd, Douglas
Lloyd, Douglas
Long, Willie
Malpass, Sidney B.
Malpass, Sidney E.
Mathews, Ramsom
McCrimmly, Jessie
McKoy, Benjamin
McKoy, Carrie
McKoy, King
McPherson, Ron
Meares, Doug
Meares, John
Meares, Roderick
Mears, Elbert
Mears, T. V
Mears, Von
Mears, Willie
Medlin, Margie
Merritt, Thomas
Miller, Buck
Miller, Hayward
Miller, Jessie
Miller, Willie
Miller, Willie
Murphy, Frank
Neal, Cricket
Owens, Dock
Patrick, Charlie
Patrick, Matt
Patrick, Steven
Patrick, Mack
Pellom, Freddie
Perkins, Harlee
Perkins, Sam
Pierce, Orrell
Porter, Johnny
Porter, Lloyd
Potter, Mack Jr.
Potter, Mack Sr.
Potter, Matthew, Jr.
Potter, Matthew, Sr.
Radford, Brooks
Radford, Buddy
Reaves, Owen
Reynolds, Burris
Reynolds, Ida
Riles, Lucky
Riley, Frank
Saulter, Arthur
Saulter, Cornelia
Saulter, Marlow
Shaw, Archie
Simpson, Herbert
Simpson, James
Simpson, James
Simpson, Oliver 'Toodle'
Smith, Charlie
Smith, Joe
Squires, Jimmy
Squires, Thadius
Sutton, Bish
Sutton, James Stanley
Sutton, Leon
Sutton, McClammy
Sutton, Miles
Sutton, Ross
Sutton, Wade
Tate, Mr.
Troy, Donnie
Troy, Jim
Troy, Joe
Troy, John Henry
Troy, Thomas
Vernon, Oscar J.
Waddell, Ed
Waddell, George
Waddell, George
Waddell, John
Waddell, John Henry
Waddell, Roger
Waddell, Theodore
Waddell, Willie
Watson, James
Weatherspoon, Eli
Webb, Fred
Webb, George
Webb, Lloyd
Webb, Susie
Webb, Susie
Webb, Walter
Wells, John
Wells, Johnny
Williams, Solomon
Williams, Alex
Williams, Archie
Williams, George
Williams, Houston
Williams, John
Williams, Julious Jr.
Wilson, Mansey
Wyche, Paul B.
Young, Joseph

Charlie Patrick of Delco taking a load of fertilizer to the chute.

FAMILY MATTERS

Shadrach Wooten and his Descendants

-- Macon Wooten, Jr.

Shadrach and Elvira Davis Wooten with their children on their Golden Wedding Anniversary. First row (left to right): Edgar, Elizabeth Wooten Powell, June Thomas. Second row: Mr. and Mrs. Wooten, Shadrack and wife, Sallie Clark Wooten. Third row: Henry and Ida McCallum Wooten, Mrs. Herbert (Mary Potts) Wooten, Cora Stephens, Willie Davis, Rose Gause Memory, Arthur Council, Jessie Wooten Council.

Shadrach Wooten was born in Edgecombe County (part of Dobbs County) in 1739. He settled in Pitt County where he built a considerable estate.

Shadrach Wooten was a member Col. Richard Caswell's Partisan Rangers during the Battle of Moore's Creek Bridge on February 27, 1776. When the Provincial Council of North Carolina met on April 4, 1776, they appointed officers for the North Carolina Regiments in the Continental Army. Shadrach was appointed an Ensign in the Fifth Regiment on April 16. On the preceding day the council adopted a resolution, in which Shadrach saw military life offered not much of a future. So he declined the commission and returned to his farm. By the time he harvested his crops, the military situation looked grime. He accepted the commission on November 23, 1776.

Shadrach married in 1763 to Elizabeth Allen, a Massachusetts girl, who came to North Carolina as a teacher. This union produced nine children who included John, Thomas Box, Shadrach Jr., Robert, Charity, Henry, Richard, and Allen.

When 1805 rolled around, Shadrach bought 1,000 acres in the Western Prong area of Columbus County. Before they moved, Elizabeth died of pneumonia and was buried at the Old Free Will Baptist Cemetery in the Sandy Bottom section of Lenoir County. After moving to Columbus County, Shadrach married a Mary Treadwell. They had no children.

In 1808, Columbus County was created out of Bladen, New Hanover and Brunswick County. Shadrach was appointed as one of seven commissioners to select a site and fund a new courthouse. Shadrach died on April 12, 1812 and was buried in Western Prong Cemetery.

John Wooten and Allen Wooten settled in Lenoir County. John represented Lenoir County in the Legislatures of 1807-1808 – 1809. Allen served one term in the Lower House of the North Carolina General Assembly, term beginning 1803.

Thomas Box Wooten was one of Shadrach's sons who moved down to Columbus County in 1805. He was born on Feb. 25, 1783 in Pitt County, N.C. He married Sarah Lucy Oliver on Nov. 13, 1804. She died in 1809. Thomas married his second wife; Mary (Duhadway) Singletary on June 15, 1809, to this union was born 10 children.

There is a story that Thomas Box and Mary, who lived on their plantation "Little Sugarloaf" on the Cape Fear River in Bladen County, figured out a way to propel tugs and boats up and down the Cape Fear by tread mills operated by horses and mules. Eventually, Thomas Box and Mary lost their fortune in this enterprise.

Thomas Box served in the Fourth Regiment, detached from the Fourth and Fourteenth Brigades of the Seventh Columbus Regiment as a 2nd Sergeant during the War of 1812.

Thomas Box married 2 more times before his death in the 1850's in Cumberland County. One of Thomas Box and Mary's sons, Robert D. Wooten, was born August 23, 1815 in Cumberland County. He married Elizabeth Morphis on August 12, 1831 in Wake County. They had 5 children: Selina Wooten, John William Wooten, Robert Alexander Wooten, Josephine "Joanna" Wooten and Mary Hodge Wooten. At the age of 35, he was made constable of Cumberland County.

Elizabeth Morphis Wooten

When the Civil War began, Robert was commissioned as a Captain of Company G ("Cumberland Rangers"), 33rd Regiment of N.C. Troops, on Sept. 12, 1861. His son John served under him. During the Battle of New Bern, on March 14, 1862, he was captured. On Sept 21, 1862, and was exchanged for a Union officer. Robert resigned his commission July 2, 1863 due to "cardiac disease". After the Civil War, he moved his family to Jones County. A few years later, he moved again to a farm in northern Lenoir County where he died on August 27, 1885.

Charity Wooten, Shadrach's only daughter, married George Reuben Grissette and settled in South Carolina.

Robert Wooten

Henry Wooten was born in 1794. He was living in Columbus County, NC, at the time of the 1820 Census. He apparently fell heavily in debt; his lands and slaves were sold via the Sheriff's office, and had lawsuits that continued through 1825. He then went westward and spent time in Shelby County, TN. Some time after 1834 he settled in Panola County, Mississippi.

Richard Wooten and Shadrach Wooten Jr. settled in Columbus and Bladen Counties. Their descendants are the Wooten's of this section. Richard represented Columbus in the Legislature at intervals from 1819 to 1861 and was delegate to the Constitutional Convention of 1861. A grandson, Major Thomas J. Wooten, was a distinguished officer of the Confederacy, as was another grandson, Brig. Gen. Richard L. Wooten and Colonel John F. Wooten of Pitt County.

Richard married Elizabeth Jane Williams in 1822.The children of this union are: Narcissa Dorsey Wooten, John Council Wooten, Elizabeth Wooten, Allen Wooten, Richard Lafayette Wooten, Sara Eliza Wooten, Rachel Wooten, Helen Wooten, Caroline Matilda Wooten, Edward Williams Wooten, Frances M. Wooten, Thomas Jones Wooten and Eliza Jane Wooten. Shadrach Wooten, Jr. married Elizabeth Treadwell, daughter of Major John Treadwell. The Wootens of Western Prong are descendants of this couple. Their children are Shadrach

Wooten III, John A Wooten, Robert Wooten, William Wooten, Mary Cromartie Wooten, Anne M. Wooten., Elizabeth C. Wooten, Charlotte M. Wooten, and Henrietta T. Wooten

Shadrach Wooten III (11 Oct 1830 – 09 Oct 1906) married Sarah Elvira Davis (15 Sep 1836 - 15 Feb 1909). Their children were John Henry Wooten, Shadrach Wooten IV, William Davis Wooten, Cora Liles Wooten, June Thomas Wooten, Walter Wooten, Edgar Wallace Wooten, Jesse Wooten, and Elizabeth. Rose Gause was their foster daughter.

Sources: *Recollections and Records of Columbus County, Story of Fayetteville, NC Troops, Our Family: A Short History of the Wooten and Related Families* by John L. Wooten.

Miller Family Migration to Bogue Township

--Stephen Carroll Pearsall

Pittman Miller was born March 4, 1844, in what was then Marion County, S. C., about three miles east of Dillon in the Piney Grove Baptist Church neighborhood. Pittman was the son of Jesse Miller and Mary Pittman of Marion County (now Dillon), S. C. During the Civil War he served as a Private in the S. C. Infantry, Company C, 26th Regiment. He also saw service with Company A, 6th Battalion Infantry and in Company D, Manigualt's Battalion, SC Volunteers. He was with those who surrendered at Appomattox Court House in Virginia on 9 Apr 1865.

In the Methodist Episcopal Church of the Thompson community in Robeson County, on October 27, 1873, Pittman Miller married Charlotte Lottie Hammond, daughter of Nathan Hammond and Harriet Thompson. Charlotte was born June 24, 1845 in Robeson County. In 1880 the family was residing in Thompson Township on the farm of Nathan Hammond. Pittman was listed as overseer. By 1900, the family was residing in Carmichael Township in Marion County, S. C. The family returned to Robeson County by the 1910 census, residing in Thompson Township. Pittman died in Bogue Township, Columbus County, on March 10, 1929 while living with his son, Benjamin Abner "Ab" Miller. Charlotte had died on January 8, 1921 on the Miller farm in Raynham, N. C. Pittman and Charlotte are buried on the Miller farm in Raynham, N. C.

Pittman and Charlotte had seven children. The first child, John Clarendon Miller, was born September 25, 1874 in Robeson County. John married in Wilmington, N. C. on June 22, 1907, Ellen Stone, daughter of Jacob Stone and Creasy Ivey of Robeson County. John died July 1, 1950 in Winston-Salem, N. C. John was buried in the Woodland Cemetery in Winston-Salem. He was predeceased by his wife, Ellen, who had died in Winston-Salem on October 14, 1937.

The second child, Guilford Preston Miller was born November 2, 1876 in Robeson County, N. C. Guilford married Hattie Ophelia Bullard (1864-1941), daughter of Alexander Bullard and Helen Hammond of Robeson County, N. C. Guilford (1876-1950) and Hattie died in Bulloch County, Georgia.

Benjamin Abner "Ab" Miller, the third child, was born August 22, 1877 in Robeson County. Benjamin left North Carolina for a short time and is listed as a "Laborer" on the railroad in Anderson Township, Indiana in 1900. He did not stay in Indiana very long and it is uncertain when he returned to Thompson Township in Robeson County. However, on December 25, 1901, in Thompson Township, he married Nancy Bogan Holcomb, daughter of James Wesley Holcomb and Eleanora Pinner of the Purvis neighborhood of Robeson County. "Ab" was a saw mill operator in the 1910 census in Thompson Township, Robeson County. By 1916, "Ab" and Nancy had moved to Bogue Township in Columbus County. At first they rented a house from the Hall family and lived on the Hallsboro road next to the John William Hall home. "Ab" was engaged in the logging and farming business. At some point "Ab" purchased land near what is now the intersection of Sam Potts Highway and Honey Hill Road. It was here, following a long period of declining health that he died on September 25, 1934 in Bogue Township.

Nancy Holcomb Miller continued to farm until her health forced her to relinquish portions of the farm. Nancy worshiped at the Hallsboro Methodist Church. Upon her death on December 26, 1953, the Reverend Richard Braunstein of Hallsboro Methodist Church conducted the services assisted by the Rev. Ronald Keyser, Pastor of Hallsboro Baptist Church. Both "Ab" and Nancy are buried in the Flynn Cemetery. Nancy was survived by a son Charles Benjamin Miller of Whiteville, a daughter Mary Sadler Miller White of Whiteville;

three brothers, Vander Holcomb of Whiteville, Charles and Frank Holcomb of Purvis; two sisters, Mrs. Sallie Thompson of Rowland and Mrs. Nellie Currie of Purvis.

Charles B. Miller was born April 5, 1916 in Hallsboro. At one time, Charles B. was employed by Farmer's Warehouse as an auctioneer in Whiteville. He was also known to "call" square dances. On September 5, 1942, he enlisted in the U. S. Army at Fort Bragg, N. C. Charles was with the XIV U. S. Army in the Southwest Pacific Area and was commended for his exemplary conduct in the field of battle. He saw duty with a 4.2" Chemical Mortar Battalion which also received commendations for its outstandingly effective support of the Infantry from Major General O. W. Griswold, commanding the XIV Army Corps and Major General Robert S. Beightler, commanding the 37th Infantry Division. Corporal Miller had the responsibility of seeing to it that the lines of communication with the front were kept clear and in good working order, regardless of the conditions that might prevail. While in the service Charles B. remarked that he sure did miss Ma's fried chicken and home made corn bread.

Charles Benjamin Miller and Dorothy Lee Arp, daughter of William Rhader Arp and Eliza (Ressie) Watts, were married at the Methodist Church in Conway, S. C. on December 25, 1945. Charles B. and Dorothy had two children: Terry Teddy Miller and Charles Marselle Miller. Charles B. took up the trade of a plumber. He was a member of the Shiloh Methodist Church in the Lee's Lake Community. Charles B. died at the Whiteville hospital on November 1, 1965 and was buried in the Shiloh Methodist Church cemetery. Dorothy Lee Arp Miller died at home in Pleasant Plain Community on November 6, 1966 and is buried in the Shiloh Methodist Church cemetery.

Mary Sadler Miller was born May 16, 1921 in Bogue Township. Her middle name came from Dr. R. C. Sadler of Whiteville, the attending physician at her birth. On January 14, 1945, in Marion, S. C., she married Clarie Dexter White, Jr. Clarie was born January 12, 1924 in Town Creek, Brunswick County, N. C., son of Clarie Dexter White, Sr., and Amma Gurganious who were originally from Pender County, N. C. Clarie had come to Columbus County and was working on the farm of Alvie Smith on Honey Hill Road in Hallsboro when he met Mary.

After the marriage, Mary was kept busy as a homemaker. They lived in the farm house that had been her parents. In order to provide for his growing family, Clarie put his clothes in a paper bag and with no shoelaces for his shoes, he hitch hiked to Newport News, Virginia. He obtained employment at the Newport News shipyard as a pipe fitter. Clarie came home on the week-ends, leaving Newport News on Friday evening. Most times he had a ride with others from the area and they would return on Sunday afternoon. This he did for a number of years. In later years, Clarie obtained a job closer to home with Dupont in Leland, N. C.

Mary Sadler Miller White, a Columbus County native, died in the Columbus County Hospital on January 21, 1981. Mary was a member of the Hallsboro Methodist Church. She was predeceased by a daughter, Tressie Lorraine White who died on February 26, 1956. Surviving children and their spouses were: Marion H. McWhorter (Frank Edward McWhorter) of La Port, Texas; Phillip Charles White (Ruth Naomi Black) of Whiteville; Nancy Holcomb White (Thelton Gleen King) of Riegelwood; Larry Dean White (Belinda Beth Todd) of Wilmington; Clarie Amma White (Robert Merlin McQueen) of Whiteville, Beverly Larue White (Ruby Mae Lynn) of Whiteville; Penny Kay White (Kenneth George Swift Lynn), Tammy Sue White, and Sandy Benjamin White all of Whiteville. Mary was buried in the Flynn Cemetery with services conducted by the Reverends C. B. Hicks and Carrie Parker.

Mary Sadler Miller White

After the death of Mary, Clarie married Ferry Gertrude Smith who was born in Brunswick County. Upon retirement from Dupont, he resumed his love of the soil and as long as his health permitted he raised corn and ground meal for family and friends. Clarie died at home in Chadbourn on April 28, 2006. He was a member of the Church of Christ in Shallotte and was buried in the Flynn Cemetery.

Mary Hattie Miller, the fourth child of Pittman Miller and Charlotte Lottie Hammond, was born April 21, 1881 in Robeson County. Mary (1881-1959) married Alexander Wesley Bullard (1863-1938), son of Alexander Bullard and Helen Hammond. Mary and Alexander died in Cumberland County and are buried at the Asbury Methodist Church Cemetery in Raynham, N. C.

Leroy Miller, the fifth child of Pittman and Charlotte, was born on April 9, 1882 in Robeson County.. Leroy married Nancy Elizabeth Arnette (1883-1957), daughter of James Robert Arnette and Laura Jane Rowell. Leroy died February 16, 1960 and Nancy died August 16, 1957. They left a large family. Marvin (1904-1907) who died young; Lacy (1906-1981), Ralph (1908-1974), and David (1910-1965) who died in Fayetteville; Bruce (1913-2004) died in Gold River, California; Lawrence (1915-1975) died in Albuquerque, New Mexico; Paul (1919-1967) died at Camp Smith Marine Base in Honolulu, Hawaii; and Philip (1921-1989) died in Livermore, California. A daughter, Nancy Arnette Miller Carlisle (1926) was last known to be residing in Danville, California. One other son, Robert Lee Miller died in 1966. Robert (1928-1966) was married to Clara Blue Bolin (1932).

The sixth child, Joseph Miller was born July 15, 1885 in Marion County, S. C. Joseph married Alice Scott. There were six children, all born in Thompson Township of Robeson County: Raymond McNeil Miller (1909-1990), Eva Lillian Miller (1912-2004) married William Melvin Long (1911-1966), Clyde Pittman Miller (1915-2002), Woodrow Wilson Miller (1917-2005), James Blaylock Miller (1919) married Ruby Ethel Tyler (1921-1999), and Elbert Monroe Miller (1922-1958). Joseph Miller was a farmer in the Raynham community and died on February 8, 1940. His wife Alice died on August 15, 1941. Joseph and Alice are buried in the Raynham Baptist Church Cemetery.

The seventh and last child of Pittman Miller and Charlotte Hammond was Coon Miller. Coon was born on July 23, 1888 in Marion County, S. C. Coon never married. He was a farmer and lived in Rowland. He died November 27, 1970 and is buried on the Miller farm in Raynham.

From Times Past: Miss Julie

--Nancy White King Pearsall

Mary Sadler Miller White, daughter of Benjamin Abner Miller and Nancy Holcomb, lived at the intersection of what is now Sam Potts Highway and Honey Hill Road between Whiteville and Hallsboro.

Julia Ward Spivey, daughter of Henry Ward and widow of Albert Eddie Spivey, was a frequent visitor to our house, and was known to the family as "Miss Julie." Miss Julie lived in a little shanty on the Powell diary farm. Miss Julie was a good woman, hard working, always wore her hair in a bun and was always welcome at our house. Mary had 9 children and Miss Julie at times helped around the house.

Once a month Miss Julie got her pension check. She would do her shopping and was known to like a taste of "spirits". When Miss Julie visited Mary she always sat in the same chair beside the snuff spittoon. One day after Miss Julie had gotten her check and had her "spirits" she stopped by to visit. She was in a talkative and relaxed mood and slumped down into her favorite chair beside the spittoon. Claire White, one of Mary Sadler's children, had just gotten a new pair of shoes. Claire had left the new shoes beside the spittoon. While Mary and Miss Julie were talking, Miss Julie, without missing a word, reached down and to the disbelief of those present, relieved herself of her snuff juice, right into one of the new shoes.

I suppose the morale of the story is that Miss Julie did not want to look down to see how high she was.

I never got to know my grandma White, but Miss Julie was like a grandmother to me. At some point, Miss Julie went to live with her daughter, Ethel. After Ethel died, Miss Julie lived with one of her grandchildren. Years later, I heard that Miss Julie died in Manetta, S. C.

Margaret Brown Wilson

Mama's Story

From the notes of Margaret Brown Wilson, daughter of Baldwin and Betty Lennon Brown, compiled by Patrica Wilson Norris, edited by Dixie Wilson Rogers, daughter of George P. and Margaret Brown Wilson.

Seated Left to Right - Pecola Jackson, _____ Inez Wayne, Linnie Formyduval, Margaret Brown, and Irene Brown
Standing left to Right, Roland Thompson, Valery J. Brown, Rhodes Wayne, Elizabeth ann Brown and Sarah Jane Brown,

On January 10, 1991, I had my eighty-seventh birthday. At 12 o'clock noon, eight members of my Sunday School class came to surprise me. They brought covered dishes and some gifts. This notebook is a gift from our teacher, Melba Wyche. So, I decided to write about a few incidents that came along with my long life. I had been the teacher of this class for about twenty years when I retired September 28, 1982. I was presented with a certificate of appreciation by our church.

I was born Margaret Brown on January 10, 1904 at Hallsboro, NC; the youngest of eight children. My father owned a farm that produced most of our food as well as food for the animals. We sold a bale or two of cotton at fifteen or twenty cents a pound to get what little money we had but we didn't need much. We only needed money for taxes and a few groceries such as flour, sugar, rice, coffee and a can of salmon for ten cents now and then; also, some cloth for dresses and underwear, sheets and pillow cases. We also had fish, squirrel and duck to eat. We burned kerosene; we didn't have electricity.

About the first thing I remember was going to Sunday School with some of my big sisters. We walked about two miles to Bogue Chapel Baptist Church at Hallsboro. There were no paved roads and no automobiles. I had a hard time trying to keep my little black patent leather slippers clean because the road was always dusty or muddy. I also remember the little white dress that I most always wore.

Mrs. Ola Pierce was my first Sunday School teacher. The beginners were called the Card Class. We received each Sunday a little card with a picture and Bible verse on the front side and some discussion on the back side. One especially lingers in my memory. It had a picture of Jesus with a lamb in His arms and other sheep following. The verse was, "The Lord is My Shepherd, I shall not want". I always enjoyed Sunday School but while my family was growing I didn't have a chance to attend much. I sent the children with neighbors and on the church bus.

Drawing of the Baldwin Brown home place.

My father, Baldwin Brown, had a farm. Not far from our house in Bogue Swamp there was a fish hole. We called it "The Big Fish Hole" because there was a smaller one nearby. When I was a little girl my father would take me fishing sometimes. I enjoyed walking through the woods. The trees would be budding out in the spring and it would smell so good. We heard the birds singing and the fish splashing in the water; a real study of God's creation. Sometimes we caught some black fish, catfish, jack and grass perch. Sometimes Father would go to Hallsboro and buy fish from John Mitchell. They would be shipped from Wilmington on the five o'clock train.

Baldwin Brown

I was eight years old when I started to school. There was a little country store just about a half mile before we got to the schoolhouse where we bought our penny pencils and five cent tablets and a few other things. I was too little earlier to walk the distance of two and a half miles, and because we had to cross over Bogue Swamp on foot logs that were higher than my head, my Mother and my sisters had already taught me to read and write. Beginning my second year, the teacher placed me in the third grade. Mrs. Ola Pierce was my teacher, a very nice person. She not only taught us what was in the book but lots of things like memorizing the twenty-third Psalm. We wrote the story of Joseph in our own words and made a little booklet of it. She taught us good manners like staying in line, not pushing and sitting up straight with our feet together and flat on the floor.

I started school in the eighth grade the day the Armistice was signed ending World War I, November 11, 1918. I stayed with my sister, Bessie, that year and school had been delayed because of a bad flu epidemic.

In August 1917, when I was thirteen, I joined the Bogue Chapel Baptist Church, later to become Hallsboro Baptist Church. I was baptized in Lake Waccamaw at Dupree Landing. We walked the two miles every Sunday to Sunday School. The road was most always dusty and muddy for there were no paved roads. All the young folks in the neighborhood would gather up and walk together.

Sometimes the Sunday School would have a fish fry at Dupree Landing. We always took a picnic basket in case the boys didn't catch a lot of fish. Our cool drink was lemonade. We took along our swim apparel and dressed behind the bushes because there was no bathhouse. I played the piano in church for some years before I married. (I still play once in a while.) I always enjoyed Mr. Charlie Rows singing a solo. One time he sang "Out of the Ivory Palaces" - I thought it was so pretty.

I was about ten years old when I road in my first automobile. Mr. Sam Black took us to Whiteville and to my first circus in his Model T Ford. There were few automobiles around until after World War I and I was about fifteen.

Henry Wayne, Rhodes Wayne, Margaret Brown. Bryon Wyche, Jim Crawford.,FR, LR. Nora Pierce, Helen Maultsby, Kate Pierce, Sally Brown, Bessie Pierce, Randolph Pierce

There were, of course, no radios or televisions. We had a phonograph and a piano. Sometimes all the young people in the neighborhood would gather at our house and play and sing and make ice cream or pull candy. This was in my early childhood. By the time I became a teenager, my sisters and one brother were all married or gone from home except my oldest sister.

When I was about fifteen years old, I helped my brother-in law, Tecumseh Pierce, harvest tobacco. His brother and his brother's two boys, Wade Hampton and John Edward Pierce, helped too. Late in the evening, we would go to Dupree and go in swimming. Hamp built a diving board for his boys out in the lake. I wanted to learn to dive and swim like they did but I was afraid. Tecumseh told me to jump off on my feet first. I did and went over my head in water. The next time, I went off head first and it was no trouble to kick the bottom and swim off. That is how I learned to swim. Some guys always had small boats tied up there and sometimes we turned one of them bottom upwards on the water so we could dive off it.

Left to Right: Carson Shaw, Irene Brown, Rhodes Wayne, Valery J. Brown, at "Weavers" Lake Waccamaw, N.C. Before 1917

One day a bunch of us were swimming in the lake and it started raining so we held the boat up over us. We were already wet in the water up to our neck. I guess we didn't want the rain pouring down in our faces.

Another day, sister Sallie's friend, Nick Chauncey, took Sallie and me, along with his brother Clarence and two sisters, Mary Lou and Annie Belle in a big motor boat to fish. We went to the river mouth (Waccamaw River and Lake Waccamaw) to see the new dam and fished all about but we didn't catch many fish. About 3 o'clock, we came back to Dupree where we had started out that day; fried our fish and ate our sandwiches. Boy was I hungry! We had our swim suits on while fishing so when we had arrived back at Dupree I got dressed and got back into the boat. Nick picked me up and tossed me right overboard. All wet again. F U N !

My life continued to be a happy one as I entered high school. Red Bug School, which was about one quarter mile behind the Red Bug Store out from Hallsboro. Miss Eliza Parker was our principal for many years. She was a very strict disciplinarian but a very lovable person. She talked and laughed with us a lot but she didn't tolerate any monkey business. She told us that our behavior reflected on our parents and she was sure we wanted our parents to be thought well of.

Our senior language teacher was Mrs. Richardson. She loved Latin and thought everybody should learn it. Before giving us an exam, she would give us a stern lecture. She often reminded us of a Bible verse that says . . . "Be sure your sins will find you out" (Numbers 32:23). We could not possibly cheat when she got through with us.

Miss Gladys West was my history teacher and my piano teacher during my senior year. For our commencement song, she taught us *"Come Where the Lilies Bloom so Fair"*. It was a beautiful song and one that was continued to be taught when some of my children were in the high school glee club. Miss Margaret Baldwin (Moyers) was also one of my earlier piano teachers.

We graduated in the first class of Hallsboro High School in the spring of 1922. We only had eleven grades then and eight-month terms. We were also the first class to get class rings and diplomas. Our school was classed as a "B" high school. We had 12 girls and two boys in that class. Lillian and Alma Pierce were sisters; Edelle and Clarkie Pierce were sisters and first cousins to Lillian and Alma; Morgan and Ruth Baldwin were sister and brother; Elbert Clemmons and Lina Ward were cousins. The rest, along with me were Margaret Merritt, Lillie Smith and Grace Carroll.

Elbert Clemmons was only sixteen years old but he was the smartest one in our class. He said one day, "I want to be rich right now; I do not want to wait on it". However, he did have to wait a while. After he graduated from the University of North Carolina, he went to work for IBM and did extremely well and did become a rich man. He gave a lot of money to Hallsboro High School, Southeastern Community College and other educational programs in Columbus County. He also helped his family a lot. He came to Columbus County sometimes when we were older and invited all the classmates out for a class reunion banquet. I saw him for the last time in the summer of 1989 at the Hallsboro Baptist Church. He had retired several years before in Tequesta, Florida and died there in 1990.

I have many happy memories of these years and will relate a few that stand out in my mind. One Saturday afternoon, Paul Sutton and I went to Lake Waccamaw to go for a swim. The water was so low we had to go a long distance before it was even knee deep. The bottom was muddy so we gave up and went back home. I dated Paul only one more time – he was definitely not my type.

While I was a senior, I dated Lonnie Pierce. This affair got its start one Sunday when I was visiting one of my friends and he was there so he took us for a ride. After that we went to our church on Sunday night to the Young Peoples Training Union. Sometimes on Sunday afternoon we rode around and visited friends. We often stayed at home. I played the piano and we sang together. There was a popular song at that time that we liked – *"Somewhere in the West"* and it went like this.

> *Is the struggle and strife, we find in this life*
> *Really worthwhile after all?*
> *Is the future to hold just struggle for gold*
> *While the real world waits outside?*
>
> Chorus: *With someone like you, a pal good and true,*
> *I'd like to leave it all behind and go and find*
> *Someplace that's known to God alone . . .*
> *Just a place to call our own*
> *We'll find perfect peace, where joys never cease, and*
> *Let the rest of the world go by.*

The melody and verses were very pretty, but as I reflect on it now, that is not the way God planned for our purpose in this life. There are many people in the world for us to love and have fellowship with. Lonnie was a very fine person. He had no bad habits such as smoking, drinking, or gambling. He would make a fine husband for a fine wife but I was not the one. He went to Florida on a vacation and wanted us to get married and go together. He was gone two weeks and I missed him very much. I didn't date him but one or two times when he came back. (I shall have to say again that he was a very fine person). He was a lifetime member of Hallsboro Baptist church with near perfect attendance. He was a World War I veteran and a mason. He had a beautiful ruby ring with the gold Masonic emblem on it. He gave it to me to wear a while but I was always afraid I would lose it so I gave it back to him. People thought we were engaged when I was wearing it.

There were a lot of others that I was associated with. While I was in school in Bolton, there was a guy who lived across from my sister, Bess. He had been in the army and sometimes he played "taps" on his bugle late in the evening. It sounded pretty but sad. I wasn't old enough to take up any time with him though. He called me Margie and gave me some music for the piano. One piece was very pretty, *"My Little Margie"*. I can only remember the chorus.

My little Margie, I'm always thinking of you, Margie.
I'll tell the world I love you.
I have bought a home and ring and everything for Margie.
You've been my inspiration – days are never blue.
After all is said and done, there is really only one,
Oh Margie, Margie it's you!

Wilbur Merritt and I rode down to the Waccamaw River mouth one Sunday afternoon from Dupree. There was sort of a road near the lakeside. I will call it a cart road, if you know what I mean. It was just a trail where people dodged trees with their mule and wagon – a hole on this side, then a hole on the other. It was so rough I wondered if Wilbur would get his Dad's car back home in a whole piece. I was in school with him in the eighth grade. He had beautiful red hair and plenty of freckles. He was so silly that I never liked him very much, so I did not date him again.

I must not forget the guy who dated two of my friends. He also dated me. One Sunday afternoon we rode down to Dupree and he asked me if I would marry him. My answer was NO! Soon after that, he took me home from church one Sunday. He told me that he and this friend of mine were going to South Carolina to be married if she didn't back out and if she backed out he would be back to see me that night. She didn't back out and that was fine with me. I have observed their married life and it wasn't anything like the nice things he talked about when he was trying to induce me to marry him. He gave her plenty of good things but too many bad things. They raised a bunch of nice children.

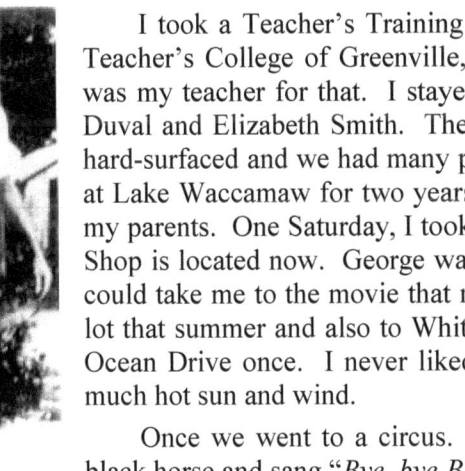

I took a Teacher's Training Course in Whiteville that was offered by East Carolina Teacher's College of Greenville, NC. I will never forget Miss Juanita McDougald who was my teacher for that. I stayed at home and rode over to school with Theresa Formy-Duval and Elizabeth Smith. The highway 74-76 from Hallsboro to Whiteville was being hard-surfaced and we had many problems taking in the detours. After that, I taught school at Lake Waccamaw for two years. I bought a model T Ford so I could stay at home with my parents. One Saturday, I took my car to a garage in Whiteville where Kramer's Ladies Shop is located now. George was there and we got into a conversation and he asked if he could take me to the movie that night. That's how it got started. We went to the movie a lot that summer and also to White Lake and Lake Waccamaw to swim. We even went to Ocean Drive once. I never liked the beach – too big, threatening and awesome and too much hot sun and wind.

Once we went to a circus. A lady dressed in black came out riding on a beautiful black horse and sang *"Bye, bye Blackbird"*. Again, the chorus is all I remember.

"*Bye, bye Blackbird*"
Pack up all your cares and woes, Here I go, singing low
Bye, Bye Blackbird
Where somebody waits for me, sugar's sweet, so is she
Bye, Bye blackbird
No one here can love or understand me,
Oh, what hard luck stories they all hand me,
Make my bed and light the fire, I'll arrive late tonight
Bye Bye Blackbird."

In 1925, I went with sister Mina, her husband and his sister, Mrs. Kate Crawford and her son Carson across the lake from Betsyburg to Council's Ridge to pick huckleberries. It is now a state park. We got lots of berries and plenty of red bugs. Coming back across the lake in those two small boats we were very frightened when a bad thunderstorm came up. It looked like we would capsize at any moment for the lake was really rough. That night, George and sister Sally and I went to Fanny Warren Smith and Gaston Best's wedding at her home. I had tried to wash the red bugs off but the bites were still there and I was miserable. I don't even remember hearing them say "I do".

On November 1, 1926, George Prosise Wilson and I were married by Judge J. B.

McIntrye in Marion, SC. George's brother Arthur and his wife, Bonnie were witnesses. We reared six girls and two boys. My life has had many difficulties and many joys as well – the greatest of these being my children. I was the youngest of a family of eight so I had never had any experience with caring for little ones. My babies were clean, sweet and cuddly. I loved them so.

I stayed very busy sewing, washing, ironing and cooking. We moved around a lot and had electricity in (Editorial comment: Pages were torn out of the original document here.)

When our youngest was thirteen months old, George went into the Navy. World War II was in progress and he spent a year in training and a year in the Philippine Islands. He was a ship fitter or plumber. We could have had plenty on the money the government sent me if there had been a good supply of groceries. Everything was scarce and sometimes when I went to the grocery store I could get only one pound of lard and sugar and many other foods were rationed. I had to stand in line at Leders Department Store to get cloth. After George was discharged from the Navy, we farmed and times were hard.

My father-in-law gave us a house and we very soon got electricity and a deep well electric pump. The light bill is now a monster – not the five cents a gallon that kerosene once was – not by a long shot!

George Prosise Wilson

During this time I made dresses, etc. for my family and neighbors. After the children were older, I worked in the alteration department in three different stores in Whiteville for 30 years. I retired at the age of 65 after working ten years at Moskow's. After retirement, I worked part-time there for ten more years; then I retired for good when I was 75 years old.

The Moskows are Jewish. One day the older Mrs. Moskow saw me reading the Bible as I was preparing to teach my Sunday School Class and she said, "Mrs. Vilson, I think you could even be a preacher". I told her," No, I don't have the talent and God wouldn't call one so little qualified; but, He wants everyone to live a life that would be a good witness of Jesus Christ."

After being a member of two large families, I now live out in the country all alone in my declining years as George had died in 1979. I enjoy visits from my children and grandchildren. I still do my driving to church and the grocery store and for visits among my neighbors.

On November 2, 1984, my foot slipped and I fell and broke my left wrist as I was going out the steps at home. It got well and looked good. On Sunday afternoon in May of the following year, I was visiting at Dr. Walter's home at Lake Waccamaw and he was glad to see it doing so well. On the very next morning, I had a check-up appointment at Dr. Munroe's and, as I was coming out the door, I lost my balance as I stepped off the curb and broke the same wrist again. I fell on the cement, broke my glasses and cut a gash in my forehead. Two security guards put me in a chair and wheeled me in the office where a nurse cleaned up my face and Dr. Munroe took me in his car to the hospital. Pat and Carolyn were waiting at the emergency entrance when we got there and took me in and Dr. Walters fixed my arm again!

On January 10, 1992 I had my eighty-eighth birthday. I have lived alone most of the time since George passed away on July 10, 1979. I can still care for myself and when I feel like it, I can drive my old car. I am careful to stay out of a great deal of traffic. I try to help our Lord take care of me. I am growing much older and do not wish to be a trouble to anyone. I am not anxious to add a lot of years to my life here on earth, only as long as I can take of myself; otherwise, I am ready to go.

Mama's Mind Exercises

When Mama (Margaret Brown Wilson, 1904-1997) was "pushing 90 " and her activities were becoming more limited, she exercised her mind in a number of interesting ways. One of these was recalling songs and tunes she had learned as a child, later as a teacher and even later as her children were young and learning new things.

I was reminded of this when my sister Margaret was on a visit home during this time and the subject of Mama remembering tunes came up. Margaret had her own little "dittie" to contribute.

"Yawning in the Mawning,
When the cowbell makes it's call
It makes me sick to get up quick
And I don't like it at all.

Oh, I wish I were in bed
With the cover's o'er my head
Instead of up and
Yawnin' in the Mawning "

This little contribution to Mama's repertoire delighted her and she could not believe one of her children had learned it so well that she could recall it 40 years later and she, herself, had never heard it. I just know she felt some pride. With eight children, you would expect that she would have missed a great deal, but I think not. She raised her children in mid-century, when life moved at a slower pace and Mothers were totally focused on motherhood.

But, I digress. Back to Mama's mind exercises: she also practiced recalling entire families she had known. "There was Miz Kate and Mr. Jim and their three girls....." She would remember where they lived, their ages compared to hers or one of her sisters, and always there was a remembered event connecting them to her life. Sometimes it was a sad recollection of a child's death; sometimes a happy school event or, who courted who, -- so many things to remember and enjoy all over again. She was undaunted by families who had eleven children-a nice challenge- just one to keep your brain tuned.

Remembering wasn't Mama's only mind exercise. She daily recorded on her calendar the current temperature at 12 noon, who visited her, what child or grandchild stopped by, when beans were planted and other happenings going on of any significance around her. It was a veritable diary, cut and dried, without personal remarks, etc. Just the facts

And, what an avid reader! She'd tackle anything. Every topic was of interest to her. Her magazine subscriptions during this time included, The National Geographic, Newsweek, Readers Digest and Guidepost. These, along with newspapers, the Bible, television and her family and friends kept her well informed.

I tell this story as it continues to happen and believe my Mother will remain alert and interesting as long as she lives, It's a testimony to a good attitude, good habits and selflessness, along with great genes, and a reminder to myself that advanced years does not necessarily have to mean "old age ".

"Now, let's see, there was Addie, Estelle, Nick and...."

--Dixie Wilson Rogers, January 1993

The Year After

--Dixie W. Rogers, April 15, 1998

This is the week that marks the first anniversary of Mama's death and it hasn't been as bad as I thought it might be. Sure, there were times when my heart ached, some tears fell; those were the low times. Most of the time, my mind was just remembering, ever so pleasantly. Strangely, I very much missed writing her every week – not because I was conscientious but I just missed being able to tell someone who cared, the trivialities of my life.

The closeness of my family played a great part in easing the pain of this year. We all shared the same degree of grief so we understood each other's feelings exactly. Mama would be so proud that her death had brought us even closer but we'd all agree that her legacy helped this happen.

Mama was so prepared to die. She looked forward to it in her last few years which very much prepared us to accept it. Some days she was grateful to the Lord for giving her extra years to enjoy her family, friends and flowers. Then, some days when she wasn't feeling good at all, she'd wonder why the Lord had not called her. Then, she'd quickly remind herself that it was His doing and He'd come get her when He wanted her. I know that many days Mama's health was far worse than she "let on" and she tried hard not to complain. Her determination to be as strong and self-sufficient as possible as long as possible was another example we won't soon forget. I suspect all of us, as I surely do, hope we can follow her example. Yet, I also suspect that each of us knows it will be difficult, probably even impossible.

Her mind! I recognize that her ability to remember details at 93 was far superior to mine at 67. This alarms me but reminds me of the mind games she played to exercise her brain and enjoy reminiscing. For instance, she'd recall a big family, usually from "The Elbow", and name them from the oldest to the youngest. Many times, she'd recall who they married and how many children they had. What a neat game! I loved hearing her work on it. Another one of her exercises was singing and reciting songs and

22 *Columbus Chronicles*

poetry she had either learned as a young student or taught as a teacher. Not the first two lines like I do, but <u>all</u> the verses. A pleasant memory I've recalled many times this past year.

I think a lot about Mama's steadfastness and how everyone who came in contact with her immediately sensed it and felt secure in it for it made for an honest and enduring relationship. Quite often, she expressed herself honestly to the dismay of the listener. It may not have been what they wanted to hear but there was no doubt about the sincerity of the statement. Right was always right with Mama, and wrong was wrong. She just did not believe in gray areas.

How I hope Mama's last three weeks were not as bad for her as we felt they were. I also hope she could feel the love and care that surrounded her completely. We were all given the opportunity to express our love and bid her goodbye, not necessarily verbally, but to have one last precious moment. Then, we will never forget what we found as we went through the house the few days after we buried her. We learned she was smarter, more organized and more thoughtful than we ever knew.

Now that a year without Mom's physical presence has passed, I'm feeling comfortable with the good memories that stay with me. My occasional yearnings to tell or show her something don't cut so deeply into my emotions anymore. We all know that her life gave us much for which to be thankful. Little did she know her relationship with us while she was here was to ease the pain for us when she was gone.

Thank you, Moma!

Old Buggy Barn at Grandpa Baldwin Brown's

Mama Said:

➢ Mama said scarves were called "fascinators" and shawls or caps were called "tippets" when she was young.

➢ Mama said: She never took to clapping in church.

➢ Mama said: When told one was sorry she was so sick her response: "Well, I'm just thankful I don't have AIDS.

➢ Mama said: When she and her cousin Howard Edwards were children, they would put syrup water in an old whiskey bottle and sit in the buggy and pretend they were getting drunk.

➢ Mama said: She used to go with her Mother to visit her Mother's sisters, Aunts Martha and Mary Brown. Aunt Martha made her a stick doll and dressed her and Mama named the doll Carrie Faircloth.

➢ Mama said: When Mr. Alva Smith got mad he always started his tirade off with, "I swear, I damn".

➢ Mama said: "Quit running through this house and slamming the door."

➢ Mama said: When she was young they played a game called "Booger in the Ditch". One person got in the ditch and tried to tag others as they jumped across. When they were tagged, they too got in the ditch – the object of the game to get everyone in the ditch as "boogers".

➢ Mama said: She felt closer to her sister Mary Lou's children than her own siblings because they were closer in age.

➢ Mama said: When Mrs. Clara Barefoot got hot in the Sunday school classroom, she would say, "It's hot enough to kill stems in here". (Curing tobacco stems in a hot pack house.)

- Mama said: She never had any children to spare when Aunt Sally, who had none, would ask her to let her have one of them.
- Mama said: When she was about 80 and in the garden with several of her daughters who were complaining of backaches, being tired, etc. "You-all let me get old first, please".
- Mama said: When she and Lollie Holmes went to Black River to fish with their dates Jack Brown, Mama's cousin, and Lon Pierce, in time they needed to use the bathroom. They went discreetly behind a dog pen. Soon, the dogs showed up and started barking. Scared the two girls to death and embarrassed them too.

"Let Me Get A Sack"

--Dixie Wilson Rogers, July, 1989

Aunt Sally Brown (1884-1964) who lived "over Bogue" was a delight to visit and, the variety of her acquaintances that made the trek down that winding road was testimony to the fact that she was pure entertainment. A bit tall, she carried herself well and her life of hard work, by her own choice, kept her lean and strong. She was my mother's (Margaret Brown Wilson's) oldest sister who never married. After her father, Baldwin Brown, died in 1943, she lived alone at the old home place for the last twenty five, or so, years of her life, living in our home her final four months, fighting a terminal illness.

Aunt Sally Brown, age 75, daughter of Baldwin and Elizabeth Lennon Brown

To get to her home, one would leave Highway 74-76 at Hallsboro, N. C. and follow the paved road across the swamp, turn right on now what is the Clyde Collier Road, and after about three-fourths of a mile, make the first right turn onto a narrow dirt road, just after Charlie Godwin's mother's two room house with a porch. No modern sign. No outlet or dead end sign necessary on this dirt road, because if you were using it, you should know exactly what is down there and where you are going. The ruts are deep but the worst can usually be dodged by taking advantage of the edge of the fields when either walking or riding. When this dodging becomes an encroachment onto Jess or Mabel Godwin's corn patch, Jess would throw some dirt into the worst of the holes, always without a grumble, we think. On past Jess's, by Ida and Dunk Jacobs', the road became some what better but their dogs were meaner. Ida would always come out the door, yelling for the dogs to "Shet up", a grand opportunity for her to see who was headed to Mis Sallie's.

Aunt Sallie always had a dog named "Pup" who barked, more to bring her up from the barn or ditch bank than to ward off visitors. Her first words to visitors were always jovial and a welcome tone in her voice and an eager look into her eyes made you know she was happy to see you and you were glad you came, a feeling that grew as you visited.

This grand old lady (she wasn't always old but always grand) was a good conversationalist without ever having taken a Dale Carnegie lesson or reading a psychologist's advice on the fine art of one on one. She was cheerful, happy with her lot, and genuinely interested in other people's lives. She always exhibited a sincere interest by listening carefully and looking one "square in the eye". She was a true lady, never asking a probing question of any one's personal affairs; taking no truck with negative gossip. With her sharp mind and varied interests, there was no lack of good conversation.

She always had things to show: beautiful flowers growing, exquisite handwork she had been working on, or maybe something she had picked up in the woods or by the fence that had attracted her attention. All the simple things about her held a fascination for her and her enthusiasm about them was always contagious.

If one ever left her yard without a gift sack, they had forgotten it. She could always come forth with some sweet potatoes, a sack of corn meal, a head of cabbage, a fresh cut of okra, a bouquet or a cutting to root; something of herself to share. Close family members were admonished to save extra bags for her so she would always have some available.

"Let me get a sack!"

--Music to my ears, and yours.

Miz' Sally's Automobile

--Dixie Wilson Rogers, January, 2008

My mother's, (Margaret Brown Wilson, 1904-1997) oldest sister, Sally Brown (1884-1964), lived "over Bogue" southeast of Hallsboro, N. C. with her parents until their death. She was always an independent character, knowing her own mind and moving forward with her life on her own terms. She was deft with a needle and thread. In fact, tailoring was her profession when she sought work off the farm. However, she could plow a row as good as any man and would never back down from any chore that presented itself. What others thought of her actions was of no concern to her as her daily life was carried out in the framework of hard work and what she knew was right.

Enter her motor car. About 1928, she bought a 1928 Chevrolet Roadster. I wish I had some detail of that purchase for I know Aunt Sally negotiated furiously as she did so in any deal in which she was involved. This vehicle had running boards, a feature that, 65 years later, has made a slight comeback. I believe they were used more for someone to catch a ride on; just a step up and hang on with your hands at the top of the door and get there in a hurry. As good as I can remember it did not have windshield wipers or a heater. Neither did it have a trunk, but the back seat could be removed when space was needed for hauling (more about that later). It did have a hand crank which was kept under the driver's seat and was used at the front of the machine when the throttle would not do the job in a slow start. Avant & Sholar, a long-time dealer in Whiteville, N.C., was probably the point of purchase. I base my assumption on the fact that when outside repairs were necessary, that's where she took it.

Sonny Boy Thurman, a mechanic at Avant and Sholar's, and from Hallsboro, was first trusted to examine the mechanism and later, David Baysden, another Hallsboro native, took over for Aunt Sally. Maybe I should have used the word "assisted" instead of "took over" because Aunt Sally was right there watching every move and asking "why" and "how much". I believe most people would have considered it interfering but not this automobile owner. Sonny Boy and David treated her with the greatest respect and seemed actually to enjoy having her around. Could it have been the novelty of a lady knowing something about a combustion engine and how spark plugs and pistons worked?

MIS' SALLY AND HER AUTOMOBILE

It always seemed we were flying along, but, of course we never went over 35 miles an hour. When, on an especially bumpy road, and there were many back in the 30's and 40's, Aunt Sally often would look back where I was perched in the back seat up close to the window and ask, "Are you keeping up?" Such fun!

Early on most days Aunt Sally had a habit of letting interesting things get in the way of her appointed rounds and we invariably found ourselves down at the "ole place" milking Pet and returning, in the dark to where she and Grandpa (Baldwin Brown) lived at that time out on the main road. Here we were, having milked in the twilight and heading home with Aunt Sally steering with her right hand and holding the milk bucket out the passenger window with her left to keep it from sloshing. I do not remember such technicalities as how gears were changed (no automatics). Where there's a will there's a way. What a fine afternoon we had enjoyed picking some blackberries, checking to see if the beans were ready, fixing a fence post, investigating a noise in the woods and walking down to the swamp garden to see if the weeds were getting out of control. At least nobody was seeing the milk adventure but there were others carried out in full view in "downtown Hallsboro" and about.

Now, onto my public experiences with Aunt Sally and her vehicle: she often stopped by our house anytime in passing to get me to go with her and, often received permission from Mama to take me home with her for a few days. Sometimes, we would go to Whiteville when she had some fresh vegetables from her garden to sell to her friends, Mrs. McKenzie, Mrs. Baggett, Mrs. Mary High and Mrs. Jennie Davis. They were such gracious "old" ladies I always felt quite comfortable around them when we drove up in the car. However, there were times that nothing could assuage my adolescent embarrassment.

A trip out to Hallsboro was always dreaded by me. At best, to be seen in that old car, with that old lady by my peers was uncomfortable. But, on occasion, she would hear an unfamiliar noise coming from the car and off the road she would pull. Out of the backseat where it was kept came the "Toe sack" and under the car it was spread. Horrors! On that toe sack Aunt Sally went. All that could be seen was a little blonde head in the front seat and two feet sticking out from under the car. She seemed always to get the problem solved and we were on our way to Pierce and Company (Hallsboro, N.C.), the local general store to purchase a remnant of fabric, some over-ripe apples at a reduced price, or maybe a plow point. Then, back by John Mitchell's store, whose specialty was ice and fish, to pick up a 50-pound block of ice. It was tied onto the front bumper of the car and we headed home as fast as we could, the ice leaving a sliver of a wet trail down the road.

Some days, our trip to Hallsboro only carried us to Mrs. Callie Hayes store to pick up some corn meal from the bag of corn that had been left earlier to be ground. Mrs. Callie was always so glad to see Aunt Sally and we would always stay a bit. Sometimes she splurged on some candy for us, but not often.

Another memorable trip was to Whiteville to the tobacco warehouse to sell her little bit of tobacco. She, of course, was a small farmer and had limited tobacco acreage. That did not stop her from making the beat possible showing she could when she sold it. The back seat of her car would come out and she carefully would pack her money making crop back there and off we would go to the market. I was not so embarrassed about getting there in this manner, but when Aunt Sally presented her tobacco for sale, I was mortified. She would get right up there in the row of tobacco so the owner of the sales warehouse and the auctioneer could see her. If it was auctioned off at an unsuitable price (to her) she'd have it moved and put on a later row to see if it would bring more. I don't remember the outcome of this switch.

Aunt Sally sold the automobile when she was in her early sixties. I do not know the details of her decision, but I do know she was having bouts with rheumatism in her right leg, which would limit her cranking, as well as quietly battling breast cancer. There had been a shortage of gas during World War II and parts were scarce. All these things probably brought her to the conclusion to sell. I believe, however, that the real reason was that she no longer was able to be in control. That would never do. I do not know of an existing photograph of this beloved jitney.

I started this story as an automobile story, but my sense is it has become another of my Aunt Sally stories. What ever it is, it is a true story, one that I have very much enjoyed all my adult life. **********

Miss Sallie Brown and Mr. Obe Young

Dixie Wilson Rogers

This picture was taken on the 4th of July in 1904 at Lake Waccamaw, North Carolina and is of Miss Sallie Brown and Mr. Obadiah Young, both of rural Hallsboro. They are on the pier, or boardwalk, in the area of the lakefront which was later to be known for many years as "Weaver's" and in the most recent decades, has had private residences fronting the lakeside there.

"The Lake" was a primary gathering place for the white citizenry of the area on this much-celebrated holiday. This gathering offered a one day break from the hard summer work on the farm. Picnic baskets were packed, for surely, everyone planned to spend the entire day socializing; only leaving the festivities in time to get home to "feed up" before dark.

The picture was taken just after "Obe" had been deputized by the Columbus County Sheriff, Sheriff Gilbert. Surely an extra deputy was unnecessary for crowd control in this day of only horse and buggy and mule and wagon. A more likely reason was to take care of a few revelers who had imbibed a little too much and, maybe a pick-pocket or two.

I was a child when Aunt Sally first told me the story of this picture and I was much impressed by that big word "deputized" that she used. It has been a part of my vocabulary from that day hence.

Aunt Sally, my Mother's oldest sister, and Mr. Young were engaged to be married. He contracted what was probably pneumonia, however, and died and was buried on or about their wedding day. She never married and told me several times that she never met anyone who she thought measured up to "Obe". She treasured, for the rest of her life, the gold wedding bands he had purchased and had had beautifully engraved with their initials on the inside. She likewise treasured the gold lapel watch he had bought for her wedding present. That too, was beautifully engraved. They remain in the family and continue to be treasured. I include this because it is such an interesting part of her life and our history.

Aunt Sally lived all her life except her last few months "Over Bogue". Mr. Young spent his brief life "up the Honey Hill Road". She lived on one side of the swamp and he lived on the other. They both have many relatives still living in the area. I treasure this photo for it brings to my imagination a simple life in great contrast to the often frenzied one we live in today. Aunt Sally told me who the lady to the left was but I cannot remember who she said. I'm better now at writing things down; I have learned my lesson.

Of course, this is my impression only as nearly as I can relate it 100 years after the event and about 68 years after I first heard it.

****

A Grapevine, a Row of Collards & a Stack of Wood

--Dixie Wilson Rogers

A grapevine, well-arbored; a healthy row of collards, free of bugs and weeds; and a cord of wood, stacked neatly, all these things in one's yard tells me one thing – somebody smart lives there.

When I visited my Uncle Charlie and Aunt Olivia Baldwin Wilson up the Red Hill Road, a prosperous farming community midway between Whiteville and Hallsboro, N. C., I pass such a sight that it brings joy to my heart. It's on the premises of our friends, Hubert and Darcas High. I knew Hubert as "Shine" when I was growing up. Later on, he went to South Carolina and found his bride, Darcas, and I got to know her.

Well, back to what that picture means to me. It conjures up lots of fond memories as well as makes for a pleasant rural scene. What fun it is to be under a grapevine eating away. Some of my maternal aunts always had grapevines, white ones, big black ones, and little red ones. I was always told that the little red ones were good cooking grapes for jelly, preserves, etc.; but growing up, I didn't care about things like that. I do believe, though, that it made the black and white ones taste better to me.

I never had a lot of fun helping saw wood or "tote it up "but a warm fire I liked. In fact my sawing ability was always "poked fun at". At one end of the cross-cut saw, you're supposed to pull your way alternately with your companion on the other end. No pushing, but don't you know it was hard for me not to push?

Now on to the collard patch. We never had many when we were growing up because Daddy (George Prosise Wilson, 1907-1979) didn't like them and he set the pace for our eating habits. But I do love them and appreciate the hard work that goes into getting "a mess "on the table. They've saved many a person in the South from going to bed hungry and they are as healthy for you as they are good.

I hope I never live long enough to see a grapevine, a collard patch and a stack of wood disappear from the passing scene. Thank you, Darcas and Hubert "Shine" for providing me of another joy in my life.

Irene Brown Shaw

Stories from the written notes of Irene Brown Shaw, 1890-1972, daughter of Baldwin and Betty Lennon Brown, and wife of Carson Shaw. Edited by Dixie Wilson Rogers

Sunday School Remembrances

Sunday School has always been the most important church organization in my life and I have always enjoyed reading my Sunday School lesson.

Barefoot, Ethel Frink -- Back Row- Irene Brown, Latha Blanchard, Mrs. Mary B. Wyche, Lloyd Ray, George Wayne at Mr. Bryan Wyche's home, Hallsboro, N. C., 1910

In the bygone days, when I was a little girl, my oldest sister, Sally, took the oldest three girls of the family – Mary Lou, Bessie and me and our brother Valery, to the Methodist Church, one mile from our home. The two oldest sisters led us across the swamp that had high foot logs (something you don't see any more), very patiently, with never a cross word. I was afraid of the water, especially dark, muddy water.

I have a special memory verse, or golden text, as it was called then – "Jesus wept". I was too young to realize just what that meant then. I know now that Jesus sympathized deeply with Mary and Martha, who had lost their only brother, Lazarus. Jesus' love for them caused him to weep. He had power from God to raise Lazarus from death so, He called out, "Lazarus, come forth" and Lazarus came to life.

Later, when we grew older, we attended the nearest Baptist Church about two miles away. The first Sunday School card was given to me by the Sunday superintendent, Mr. Henry Wyche. The "Golden Rule Text" was taken from Revelation 1:18, "I am he that liveth, and was dead; and, behold, I am alive for evermore, Amen; and have the keys of hell and of death."

When I was older, a son of Mr. Henry Wyche was our teacher and superintendent. I found the study of the Bible, along with its literature very fascinating and interesting, therefore I studied diligently.

Before I was 18, I was elected as teacher of the Junior Sunday School class which was composed of boys and girls. This I found very enjoyable as well as educational. For 6 years, I was organist at my church. On August 27, 1907, I presented myself for baptism and was baptized into the church at Dupree Landing at Lake Waccamaw, about one and one half miles from my home. I was baptized by the Reverend Angelo Porter, brother of Dr. Samuel J. Porter. Dr. Sam was a missionary to South America and was pastor of a church in Washington, D. C.

My first mission work was to collect money to send to the foreign mission field in China. It seems that money was scarce but every little bit helped. I asked a man for a donation and later he gave me a quarter. I guess he felt sorry for me or gave it to get rid of me. I heard later he was a Catholic. When the time came to turn it over to the church, I had nearly five dollars. The other three girls did not have as much as I did. So, such is life.

In my childhood days our first Methodist pastor was a Mr. Betts, the next The Reverend A. J. Porter, then The Reverend J. M. Marlowe and The Reverend Vale. Our Baptist pastors, as I remember them were, The Reverend T. J. Cobb, The Reverend W. S. Ballard, The Reverend Angelo H. Porter and The Reverend Roland Hedgepeth. At the close of Reverend Hedgepeth's pastorate at Hallsboro, The Reverend Frank T. Wooten served us for five years, then came a Mr. Campbell and others. For some reason, I thought these ministers were men of great courage and very Christ-like.

My Experience as a Teacher

During one's life, many changes can be made that will add a lot to a person's environment and advantage. My advancement came about gradually. In 1912 our county superintendent of the public schools asked me to teach in a school three miles from my home. I really did not have all the preparation I needed for this, but I kept on trying to do my best. The harder I tried, the more I felt my incompetence. Each summer I attended a six-week summer school some place until I secured a first certificate. I was very proud to have this in those days, and still am until this day.

The first two years of my teaching experience were in a one teacher school. The grades ranged from one through seven and between twenty-five and thirty pupils registered. Bad weather prohibited regular attendance. Some had to walk a mile though ice, slush, rain or whatever. I, myself, lived three miles distance and when the weather was too bad, Father would take me there in the horse and buggy and return for me in the afternoon. (I always thought he and Mother were good and quiet parents. They enjoyed life with us, I thought, more than any other parents who lived near us). Cars were not available then as now, so we thought nothing of the long walk. It took only one hour to walk three miles. We had our raincoat, overshoes, umbrella, and a kerchief or hat for our head. In meantime, there was no need for complaining. I have some of these pupil-friends who still live in the area even today. They were all well behaved young people.

In the school year 1914-15, I taught the first four grades in a two-teacher school nearer my home and for a smaller salary. This I enjoyed more because my responsibility was less and my principal was a wonderful lady, Miss Dora Blake. Most of the time, my older sisters accompanied me to school part of the way, as they were in high school.

The children in this school were unusually good and well-behaved. One fourth grade boy was educated for a teacher and later became a professor and a principal of several schools; now he is close to retirement age. Two of his sisters were teachers. Several of these pupils became businessmen. Many are progressive farmers which is a most worthwhile occupation and a very necessary vocation.

In the 1915-16 school year I was asked to teach four months in a school where the teacher had been discharged for his heavy drinking. (I didn't know him). I didn't realize what I was up against, but somehow must have made a reasonable impression, for things worked out nicely and I was asked to teach again the next term, which I did not accept. This was my fourth year of experience. I realized some pupils didn't know the meaning of school, yet some did and made good. Some parents move from place to place so often that the children could not become adapted to the environment. I didn't consider myself a splendid teacher, but, to help a teacher be a good one parents must cooperate to help bring out the best in <u>all</u> children.

Pierce School, Hallsboro, N.C.
Fifth Row, L-R: Sally Brown, Mary Lou Brown
Sixth Row, L-R: ----, Bryan Wyche, Jim Wyche
Second Row, on Rt. Bessie Brown, fourth from left Mina Brown

The next year, I accepted the first three grades in a two-teacher school where, again, my responsibilities were not as great as a one-teacher school. This was an excellent group of children; well behaved and of good parentage, just a good neighborhood all around. These were people who attended church and were very civic-minded.

Mr. F. L. Wooten, our Superintendent of Public Instruction was a man of unusual ability, a keen mind and clean heart. This made him a man of honesty and much loved by everyone. Miss Eliza Parker of Garner, North Carolina was Columbus County School Supervisor. She was a wonderful lady who really belonged in a classroom. We loved her and anticipated her visits with us. The principal was Professor H. N. Kelly; a man who was quiet, very capable, and always stood for the right.

My sixth year of teaching came about in a peculiar way, since I had married at the end of my fifth school year. I was happy to think I would be a farmer's wife, but on April 6, 1917, the United States declared war on Germany. On September 20, 1917, my husband was called to service for his country as were thousands of other men. We were very happy, and planning ahead, had purchased furniture and set up housekeeping. Of course, we were both very disappointed that he was called into service, but we closed our doors and I went home to my parents. I helped them with their work until my husband was given an honorable discharge in April, 1919, too late for us to farm that year. He accepted a job at the Boardman Lumber Company, tallying lumber under John Tudor.

After thirty years of housekeeping as a farmer's wife, I accepted a third and fourth mixed grade in my hometown in an 18 to 20 teacher school. This was very interesting in many ways.

I thought this group of children should be divided into four groups. Even the most mischievous was a lovable youngster. They were somebody's sons and daughters.

One day I told them I loved every one of them, and one little fellow asked, "How can you do that?" That can be easily done if you apply a lovable attitude in most cases. But you must study a child carefully and figure out his or her need, and, if he is neglected, he is sure to know it. Every child needs special attention and when they can get the best attention, they can make better progress toward receiving an education. Children, as well as grown-ups, like to be loved. Just think how much the short word "love" can mean to anyone.

I found, in teaching everyday, we need to emphasize and live for the Lord. My first devotional was taken from John, Chapter I, "The Word". Also, one needs to be mission-minded. The story of Joseph blends in school life very closely, as does the story of the prodigal son. Also, Jonas' experience creates a great deal of interest. Right here I will say all teachers should be Christians in order to lead the children in the right way.

Redbug North Carolina Remembrances

In the summer of 1905, a Mr. W. E. Broderick conducted a pay school in the Alliance Hall for about one or two months duration in a neighborhood across Bogue Swamp which had a post office known as "Redbug". Professor Broderick had taught the school term before in the Elbow neighborhood about two miles southwest of Hallsboro.

At the close of the pay school at Redbug, Mr. Broderick put on an all day program and a night program. The people of the surrounding neighborhood served a picnic lunch. After the lunch, the Governor gave us a wonderful talk on education. After the speech, there were contests. There was one I remember especially. There were a number of long strings fastened to a post and each contestant was to test his skill by getting all the string he could in his mouth – not using any means in taking it in except his mouth. Bennett Ray won the prize. All this and the night program was a very enjoyable occasion.

Tedder School

In 1905-06, a school was organized and called, "Redbug School District 5" and classes were held in the Farmers Alliance Hall in Redbug. Another building there was known then as Pierce and Company. A teacher was hired – Miss Mabel Goode of Cleveland County, North Carolina. She was a graduate of Oxford College, North Carolina, and weighed about 98 pounds. She had eighty pupils from first through the seventh grades in this room which, perhaps 20 x 30, and had five months of school.

It scarcely had sitting space and we had to recite just where we sat. The beginners were put in a corner and an elder boy heard them recite their lessons. Crowded was the name.

Miss Goode certainly had good control of all pupils. She corrected and punished when she saw fit. Her rules were few but we knew to respect them and everything went well as could be expected.

In autumn of 1907, the new building had been finished and we attended school there. Miss Goode was again principal and teacher of the higher grades. A Miss Ola Caldwell from Spartanburg, S.C. was Miss Goode's assistant teacher. They were two wonderful teachers (1907-08).

Old Evergreen, NC

--By Irene Brown Shaw

An Oral Reminisce

Evergreen, North Carolina was once known as Illion. Illion was the post office but later the name was changed to Evergreen because of the evergreen shrubbery one mile east at the home of Mr. Ashley Benton, who was instrumental in having the name changed. Mr. Benton was a very helpful citizen of this section.

Before the Atlantic Coastline Railroad was constructed through Evergreen the mail was delivered by horseback from some other post office, perhaps Cerro Gordo or Fair Bluff, and then on to Bladenboro, Lumberton and other points. Not being thickly settled, and because of poor roads or perhaps trails, the mail was not delivered more than once or twice a week. At that time, people worked for twenty-five cents per day; boarded themselves, without complaining.

In the year 1808, Bladen County was divided and the south side was called Columbus County in honor, of course, of Christopher Columbus who was instrumental in discovering North America. The northern part remained Bladen County. Tatum Township became part of Columbus County in which Evergreen is located. It was named for a Mr. Tatum who owned and operated a turpentine distillery in Evergreen, or perhaps Illion, as it was named at that time.

There was once a store here that was known as the Illion Supply Company. The men who formed this company were Gaston Williamson, F. Marion Stephens, and Simpson C. Fields. Will C. Thomas, Mr. Field's son-in-law, was general manager. The store stood on the south side of North Carolina Highway 74.

Evergreen Churches

The first church built in Evergreen was the Missionary Baptist Church and stood near Highway 141, about one-fourth mile from the crossing at the big oak. The north side of highway 74 was then known as Griffin Crossroads, named in honor of Mr. Frank Griffin and his son, Columbus.

Ashley Benton was a help in organizing the First Methodist Church of Evergreen, North Carolina. It was built one mile east of the Atlantic Coastline railroad by the highway NC 74. This site was in front of the Methodist Cemetery, very close to Ashley Benton's home. In 1958 a new house of worship was built in Evergreen on the north side of NC 74.

The Baptist Church was organized in 1879 as Griffin's Crossroad, but the name was later changed to the Evergreen Baptist Church. In the registry the years from 1892 to 1901, records included names such as Orrie Lennon, who died November 1, 1901 or before; Ann R. Lennon, who died in 1901 or before; Hannah H. Lennon, who married Enoch Nance of Chadbourn, and died later; Sallie J. Lennon, who died in 1895. The list of male members show the initials given as R. Y. Lennon (Rosser Yates), G. P. Lennon, J. P. Lennon and J. I. Lennon. There are fifteen listed. The real names, such as Oscar Wright and Gaston P. are the only ones fully written. (*Notes on the bottom of the page listed names, Dennis Stephen Lennon, son of Lott B. and John Cale Lennon. Information inconclusive. Ed*)

Dennis S. Lennon, Jr. and John Cale Lennon were among the first Sunday School Superintendents of Griffin's Crossroads Baptist. John Cale Lennon was the grandfather of Mr. Hartford D. Lennon. The church was torn down and rebuilt at the present site in the 1930s. In the 1950s an educational building was built in back of the old sanctuary, trusting that soon they could build a new sanctuary, baptistery, and extra rooms for classes. The first service was held in the new sanctuary the first Sunday in September, 1957. By the first Sunday in October, 1958, there was money enough on hand to lift the indebtedness. The note was burned at the night service the third Sunday in November, 1958. It is believed that Carson Powell, David Dow, and Jim Dixon preached the first 14 years in this new church.

The Wonderful Big Oak of Evergreen

According to tradition, there was a big oak tree in the corner of Mr. J. C. Parkin's yard that was over two hundred years old when it was destroyed. The big oak stood where North Carolina Highways 74 and 242 cross and was the voting precinct for many years for Tatum Township. (Mrs. Parkin was a daughter of Mr. Ashley Benton. Mr. Parkin passed away in 1962.)

The oak stood for many years and was a beautiful sight. Planted and grown by our Lord and treated kindly by man. I have never heard its age discussed yet through the years it stood the test of life, such as storms, droughts, rain and freezing and hot temperatures. It has also sheltered many from the heat of the sun.

When Highway 74 was hard-surfaced in 1926 through Evergreen, the "Big Oak" was left to stand as a memorial to the surrounding neighborhood. Therefore, a curve that was required in order to let this tree stand.

In the latter part of 1960, the North Carolina Highway Commission decided the road through Evergreen should be improved and widened so they disposed of the "big oak". Some thought the great oak should have been preserved as a monument in the town of Evergreen or to the whole township of Tatum.

Tradition has it that there are, or were Indian Mounds near Evergreen on the east side of Highway 242 and north of Highway 74. A longtime, older resident told me about this.

An Evergreen Story Remembered

Mr. Vance Fields told this story to Irene Brown Shaw during the 1960s.

Dennis Lennon married a girl and just before the birth of the child, one morning while she was cooking breakfast, a horse put his head in the window and frightened her to death. The window must have been a wooden shutter that had been left open for fresh air. After this experience, Dennis S. Lennon never married again.

1952 Evergreen Baseball Team

This picture is of the 1952 Evergreen Eagles summer baseball team. Pictured kneeling: Batboy, Bill Johnson. Bottom row: Coach William O. "Bill" Johnson, Billy Brooks, Dan Bartley, Ted Inman, Will Nance, "Peanut" White, and Denver Lennon.. Top row: Jerry Johnson, Tommy Lewis, Tommy Edwards, Leggett Johnson, Billy Britt, Charles Branch and Thomas Ray Johnson. Submitted by Betty W. Branch

Vance Fields' Story

Mr. Vance Fields was born on December 29, 1874. He told this story in Evergreen, North Carolina to Irene Brown Shaw in June, 1965.

-- Patricia Wilson Norris

When I was a boy as early in life as I could, I worked at a big lumber mill until after I was married. I learned any kind of work that was to be done. Up until the time I was married I made 30 cents per day.

Short and Beers Lumber Mill, Hallsboro

From the time I left home early in the morning I worked twelve hours a day. That would give me approximately $2.40 a week. For a long while we were paid two times a year: Christmas and the first of July. Later I was paid by the month. When we were paid twice a year it seemed a long time between pay days.

Until I was married at twenty years old, my father would go to the office and get my money and use it as he saw fit. One day I got married and went early the next day to get my pay – soon after I was paid. My father went in to get it and there was none for him. The bookkeeper said, "I am glad you are married, and, if you need some money I will lend you $25.00". That was a large amount of money for me to borrow so I declined the offer.

I did not have anything but my wife. Her people and mine didn't let us have anything that was ours; not even our clothes – just what we had on was all we had. I purchased some cloth known to everyone as homespun. It cost five or six cents per yard and was used for sheets, pillow cases, under clothes and other items. My wife made these garments by hand.

In those days cotton, as you know, was grown, picked by hand and then carded into small rolls to spin into thread on a spinning wheel; then woven into cloth on a handmade loom. Almost all garments were handmade.

Wool from sheep, after being sheared, was washed and treated in like manner, to be knit into socks, headpieces or woven into cloth to make coats and pants for men and boys and for other uses. Wool was washed and pulled so it would be easier to card into rolls, or batts, for padding quilts. The roll of cotton or wool varied according to the size of thread desired.

You wonder about coloring or dyeing? Brown sheep wool needed no dye stuff. In those days many people were skilled in the art of dyeing cloth at home. Walnut hulls, oak bark were good to use to make dye and broom straw and laurel leaves made yellow. Indigo plants were grown at home for blue. Although there were some factories, people then knew much about mixing colors to get the desired shade.

When our first baby came we had two quilts my wife had made that we used through the hard, cold winters. We named the baby Frederick. A friend gave us two quilts, so my wife used them on the bed and I took the two we already had and put them on the floor and slept there.

I had made our bed with wooden 2x4 lumber and floored it with boards that I could get. Then, someone gave me 25 pounds of cotton for a mattress which was very thin but we appreciated it very much. It will be surprising to young people of today to think about such a crude bed;

two by four lumber framing for the bed and boards to hold up the thin bedding we had accumulated.

We were happy trying to work, take care and have something. I purchased a pair of overalls and wore them until they were in rags. We lived in a one-room little shack in what is still known as the "Sooky Field". Since then, I have built seven houses in my neighborhood, each one a little larger than the one before.

Later, when I had accumulated a little more, my wife's parents took notice and came to visit us. Finally they offered to help but I let them know we didn't need any help from them. I told them we could manage our own affairs. All along, now and then, they would come for a visit and one day they told me that they liked me better than any son-in-law they had. They also said they thought I knew better how to manage to get ahead than most men.

My! It was hard times! However, nothing can be so hard, or bad, that it doesn't have some good points. In the meantime, my wages was raised to 60 cents per day. That was getting somewhere, sure enough, in those days.

Let me tell you, the "Cleveland Panic" came along and no one knows how hard the times were except those who experienced trying to live and let live through them. It was like enduring hardness as a "good soldier", although at that time, we were not soldiers of the army – just men working and battling for and with life, honestly and our families.

Today, I can look to God and say, "How Great Thou Art". You just don't know the things I have been through.

I have also mixed mortar and laid millions of brick. I guess my health has been usually good through these years and, on the 29th of December 1964, I was ninety years old.

The period of time in which I have lived has changed more than younger people realize and, after all, I feel quite sure that I have lived during the best period of history. Now all my children are parents and grandparents, even great-grandparents.

I still live in the same community in which I have lived until now or since childhood. I live now, with a son and his wife, in a house I built years ago.

My wife has been gone ten or fifteen years and I have missed her very much. I have enjoyed people and friends and also my church work, as well as many other things.

Wm Byron Pension

State of North Carolina S S.

Robeson County

On this 28th day of April AD 1855, personally appeared before me a Justice of the Peace in and for the County & State aforesaid Sarah Inman aged 65 years resident of Robeson County in the state aforesaid, who being duly sworn declares that she is the widow of William Bryan deceased who was a private in the Company Commanded by Capt. Cale Stephens in the regiment of Volunteers Commanded by Col. Moore in the War declared again Great Britain by the United States 18th June 1812, that her said husband William Bryan, volunteered at Whiteville in the State of N.C. on or about the 1st day of Sept 1814, for the term of Six Months, and was honorably discharged at Greenfield, NC on or about the 1st day of March 1815 as will appear by the muster rolls of said company. She further states that she was married to the said Wm. Bryan at her residence in Columbus Co. NC, on the 6th day of May 1819 by one Jonathan Bryan, a Minister of the Gospel & that her name before her said marriage was Sarah Baldwin that her husband died at his residence in Columbus County on the 30th day of Nov, 1820.

She further states that she was married to Hardy Inman at Whiteville, N. C. on the 25 day of Sept 1827 by one Wm Camp a Magistrate & that her said husband Hardy Inman died at his residence in Robeson County N. C. on the 26th day of Feby 1840, & that she is now a widow.

The foregoing declaration & affidavit were sworn to & subscribed before me the day & year above written & I certify that I know the affiant to be a credible person that the claimant is the person She represents herself to be & that I have no interest in this claim.

Benj. Freeman J. P.

--Submitted by Sam West

TALES OF COLUMBUS

Submitted by Lou Floy Watts Milligan

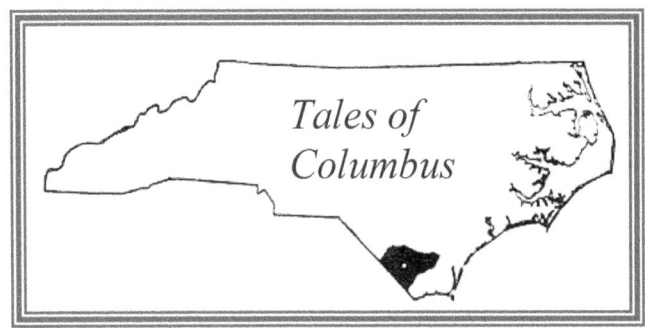

Preacher Crance Hardee

Preacher Crance Hardee was a legend in his own time. He preached everywhere all the time, and what a memory he had - the entire Bible, events and dates of his life. Preacher Crance and his wife Kathleen Mishoe celebrated more than sixty years of marriage and had five girls and two boys.

He said that he got under convictions in 1947. He got so he could not eat or sleep. He went to Glendale Baptist Church and went to the altar. He asked God to forgive him for all his sins and save him. God said,

"**I give you salvation. I give you a new heart! I remove your sins as far away as the east is from the west. I will not even remember where your sins went.**"

The heavy burden was lifted. He was overjoyed and filled with love and freedom...even the trees had a golden glow.

Some time later he was in the field plowing when the mule refused to go. Mr. Crance could not get the mule to go, so he sat down on the plow. Then God said to him,

"**Go preach my word!**" Mr. Crance answered; "I am just a poor farm boy with a mother, a wife and two children to care for. I don't have any education or any nice clothes."

Later he was walking across the field in front of his house, when it felt like something had stung him on his hip. There was such pain and swelling that he barely made it to the house. Someone carried him to the Loris Clinic. Dr. Rogers asked him how he could have hurt himself so. Two other doctors looked at the x-ray; one was from Charlotte and one from Florence. His hip bone was crushed, and there was a four-inch split in the bone, and all the muscles were pulled from the bone. He could only cry, pray, and holler that he wanted to go home. When he got home, his wife told him that the twins had pneumonia.

When the revival came again to Glendale, he told the people that God had called him to preach. Eric Gaskin was the pastor, and Lorenza Todd was the guest speaker. There was praying, preaching, shouting at that revival. Preacher Crance asked God for gifts, and God said, "**You have the gift of the laying on of hands, of healing, go and use that.**"

He was saved in 1948, licensed in 1950 and ordained in 1951. Preacher Crance fixed up a prayer room in a tenant house, and years later had one in the pack house. He spent many hours there in solitude, prayers listening to gospel music and preaching on the radio. He himself preached over the radio. This man was known and loved by thousands of country and small town folks in the Carolinas. If people did not hear him at church or on the radio they heard him at many funerals. What a devoted man of God!

Harvey Powell

Harvey Powell, born about 1906, was the son of Vester and Mary Watts Powell of the New Life Church Community, three miles east of Tabor City. His mother inherited a nice farm and they had a large house. Harvey had one brother and four sisters. Harvey's mother Mary was crippled with rheumatoid arthritis and was bent at the waist parallel to the ground. This did not stop her from all her many duties at a wife, mother, and farmer. Tragedy struck this family. Two of the sisters were struck with arthritis after they were grown; one was drawn so that her chin was padded to keep it out of her chest. The entire family came down with typhoid when the epidemic came through. Young Harvey was the only one able to doctor and feed this very sick family.

Then another tragedy struck. When Harvey was about sixteen, he fell at a warehouse and broke both legs. When the cast was removed, his legs would not bend; he got around on crutches the rest of his life.

December 2008

Harvey had to use his brain and guts to make a living and became ambitious. He bought a little store from his uncle and began running the store. He had the usual drinks, nabs, bread, and gas, but he also bought bonded whiskey from near by SC and sold it. Hanging around the store, he became pretty good at playing poker with the boys. His store became the hang-out place for all boys and men and especially bachelors. Harvey had no trouble getting young boys to drive him to bigger poker games in two states. He had no problems winning all the men's tobacco cropping money. Some of the women in the neighborhood reported him to the sheriff for selling whiskey, but it would be hid in many cars by the time the sheriff came. One time his cousin Sim took a sack of jars and ran across the field when the sheriff stopped; this gave others time to hide the whiskey. Harvey made a lot of money and was able to buy many farms and build a nice house. When some neighbors were desperate for another drink, Harvey would buy their farm or tractor.

Harvey was a good talker and prosperous and married a young pretty, smart girl from across the woods. They had three children who have done well and many of his grandchildren are professionals and big farmers. Harvey's one sister who married never had any children.

Once there was a big scattering of a store full of laughing men. Two neighbors were mad at each other and one went home to get his gun. Without knowing this, one of Harvey's young sons threw down a loud firecracker on the doorsteps. When this loud noise sounded, they all just knew that the man came back shooting. Some went under the counter; some broke down the back door; some knocked down other people and went out other doors.

There was another incident that kept people talking for years. There was a poker game at the Mill Pond at Tabor. Bruton and Spivey shot and killed each other. Harvey had a rough time finding his crutches and left with only one. Someone ran into an open car door, peeling it back on the hinges; another pulled the choke out all the way on their car; another was offered a ride and replied," No, I don't have time, I'm in a hurry."

A Miracle for Cousin Kit

Kit Rogers, a special cousin who had always been honest and special to me, told me often about God and his healings. Kit spoke openly and honestly and you always believed her sincerity. One day she told me of an awesome miracle.

"The Holy Spirit or Spirit of Truth has always given me answers and talked to me. I have been healed from many afflictions. I started reading the Bible more instead of looking at the soap operas after a voice told me, "Don't grieve the Holy Spirit!"

The night before I was to have a tooth filled, I talked to God, "God, You are all powerful: You have healed my body of many illnesses. If you can heal diseases, you can fill my tooth." The next morning as I dressed to go to the dentist, I pried and pried at my tooth, trying to get out what I thought was some particle of meat lodged from breakfast I was shocked to find that the tooth had indeed been filled.

I still kept my appointment. The dentist's wife happened to be in his office. When I told her, she cried out, "'I have been praying for a miracle so my unbelieving husband would believe!" The dentist confirmed that my tooth had been filled. I asked him if it had ever happened to any of his clients before. He replied that one man told him that his tooth had been filled with a gold filling by God."

Maxine Wright Mumaw

There was a blood clot in my brain and I died. I was falling through a dark tunnel, burning up. I yelled for everyone to take their hands off me. I realized that I was going to hell. I prayed with all my might! I had been taught about Jesus and had Him in my head, but not in my heart. I saw my deceased Dad's face, and he was so sad but did not say anything. I was terrified. Then a voice said," Do not be afraid, I am right here with you." From that moment, I started traveling toward a brilliant light and the most beautiful rainbow colors. What peace! What joy! But there was a pounding on my chest, and the military doctors were giving me the electrode shocks. After this, I was in a coma for twenty-two days. I could not move or make a sound, but I could hear everything that went on in my room. Those military nurses were cursing terribly. The first people that I witnessed to were those cursing nurses. Later I went far and near telling people about my experience of heading to hell, and **then meeting Jesus!!!**

Calvin Soles

As told by Cainey Spivey

Charles Calvin Soles was one of twelve children. He married Annie Jean Gerrell. He was father of Duff Soles, grandfather of Charles Soles, great-grandfather of Wallace and R.C. Soles, Sr., and great-great grandfather of well-known N.C. Senator R.C. Soles, Jr. This name has been prominent in Tabor City for over one hundred years. The C.C. Soles and Company had several stores in Tabor City. Hundreds of area farmers did their yearly trading and charging at these stores.

One story told on Calvin Soles was that he was with seven other Confederate soldiers trying to get home after the war. They had to swim across a river: some praying, some cursing, some drowning. Mr. Cainey Spivey told this story. Calvin was a bragger; he like to boast and fight. At the Iron Hill Store where Lawson "Loss" Wright was clerk, some men were gathered after a long day of working on the road. They were tired and started drinking. Calvin got to chasing Loss around in the store aggravating Loss, and Loss kept begging him to stop. Finally Loss shot Calvin; the bullet lodged in his arm or shoulder.

Years later Calvin was down at the beach where they were unloading barrels of fish. To impress the black men about how strong he was, Calvin was tossing the barrels like firewood. This action caused the bullet to come lose and kill Calvin!

Joshua Long

As told by Cainey Spivey

Joshua Long married Mary Eliza Alford, daughter of John B. and Dolly Carroll Alford. After they had about five children, Mary Eliza died young. These children were raised in different families. Some of the girls had hard lives and had to become strong women.

Later Joshua married a Rabon woman. One day when Josh came home, he found his wife down the garden path with another man. Josh got his shotgun and filled them both with buckshot. Josh's father-in-law was mad and came riding up to the house on his horse and they had a shoot out.

Joshua had to go to court in Conway. During court, the judge called a court helper up to the bench and the man left the courtroom. The man came back later with a bag for the judge. When it came time for the judge to sentence Josh, he handed Josh the paper bag, and said, "This is a bag of more buckshot, go home and use it if you need to."

William Stedman Porter

Stedman Porter was the first born son of James Albert and Balzura Wright Porter. He was born in 1882. He was a good-humble fellow who helped his father work the farm and raise lots of animals. He did lots of hard work clearing new ground, planting, harvesting, and building.

As a young lad, he liked to go hunting. One day he was hunting in Aunt Lydia's ole bay and got lost. This gave him post-traumatic-syndrome, and he was sent to a hospital in Raleigh. He told that he had rather die than go back. They had put him in a tub of water and put electric probes to him.

While yet a young man, he was walking to Iron Hill's one room school about two miles away with his siblings and cousins when he fell into the icy water of Little Iron Hill Run. The students had to cross an ice-covered foot log and Stedman slid. He was wet and upset and said a curse word. He knew his parents would really be upset; he promised his co-walkers if they would not tell his parents that he would never say another curse word. Everyone thinks he kept his word. He married and had a nice house and out buildings, took in many into his home, and raised Carl Edwards and Maggie Mae, an infant. On Sundays he enjoyed going to his Primitive Baptist Church and sitting at the wood pile and picking out black walnuts.

Susie Long Boswell

As told by Cainey Spivey

Susannah (Susie) Long was the daughter of Joshua and Mary Eliza Alford Long. Her mother died when the children were little and they were raised in different families. These children had it rough and Susie grew up to be a strong-willed woman.

Eli Boswell, a confederate veteran who liked to drink, was a dark-skinned man with dark eyes and hair. During a party at the Dow Fipps Farm, he and Riley Spivey got to fighting about a dog. Eli cut the jaw-bones out of Riley Spivey. Eli was sentenced to hang.

Independent, spirited Susie dressed down to her shimmy and married Eli at the gallows. He was then branded instead of hanged.

Susie probably wished later that she had let him hang, after he deserted her with several children. As Susie plowed the oxen, the knee-baby tried to nurse her. She raised turkeys to sell and it took her two weeks to take the turkeys sixty miles to Wilmington to sell. To feed her children she became a midwife. She had a steady job of this since almost all the women had a baby every two years. For pay, she got lots of food, including smoked hams, from the proud parents. Susie tried to scare away the older children when the new baby was due. She made them think she was a witch and could do wonders. Once while delivering one of Anna Wright Fowler's 15 children, she stuck a fork into a stump and milked a glass full of milk from the fork. Her niece, Mime Hodge of the Fowler Town Community, was also a midwife and lived to be about 104.

Someone said that Eli always wore a bandanna on his head to hide the brand. One of his grandsons said that he was branded on the hand.

Armegy R. Soles

(A story passed down)

Armegy R. Soles, born about 1849 to Jordon "Jird" and Anna Eliza Watts Soles, was one of twelve children. Armegy had many stories told about him through the years. He married first Sarah Norris, daughter of William, Jr. and Priscilla Alford Norris. Sarah had son James Barliver "Bud" who went to Georgia, and Sarah "Sis" who married Kenyon Wright and later lived near Bladenboro. When first wife died, he married Martha Louvina Cox, daughter of Isaac and Molcey Stanley Cox. Martha had several children, including two sets of twins. Then across the ditch in a tenant house lived Kit Ward, who reportedly had several children for Armegy. Tradition was that Armegy was the father of thirty-five children?

This story was passed down about Armegy. In his older age, he watched the person who shaved him and saw where he put the straight razor. Armegy got up and cut his throat. After his throat was cut, he sat down and enjoyed his last chew of tobacco before he died.

Beth Bruton

Beth Spivey McMillan Bruton was one of ten children of John "Furney" and Kitsey Bell Jacobs Spivey. This family was living in Tabor City; and her dad, three sisters and a brother worked at the Tabor City Crate Factory. This was a big industry when farmers were planting vegetables for market and growing lots of strawberries. Beth's father got killed in a wreck when the twins were three years old. Beth's mom decided to move back to the farm in the fall of 1934. Neighbors helped her with farming advice. Beth was plowing one mule when she was twelve and her brother Joe plowed the other. In 1944 four of Beth's brothers were in service. Norman was in army nine years and saw the prison camps as the Germans retreated. During the war, Beth went to Wilmington and welded for four years. Beth's mama decided to move back to town. The family was excited to finally have indoor plumbing.

Beth married John McMillan and they had one son. Beth worked hard all those years with her husband and raised her son. Years after John died, Beth married truck driver Bill Bruton. Beth bought out her brother's coffee shop in Tabor City and ran a successful restaurant for eighteen years; also helping raise four grandchildren next door. Beth had an amazing personality, drawing repeat customers to her restaurant. She was so fun-loving that all folks thought they were her special friend. After she retired to her lovely home and beautiful yard on the Vinegar Loop Rd, people begged her to come to town each day and just visit. What a spunky lady: plowing a mule, welding a ship, and running a popular restaurant.

Hance Wright

Hance Wright was son of Simpson and Prudence Norris Wright. He was named after his Uncle Hansen Wright who went north to fight the Yankees and never came home. Hance had his own farm because his dad bought land from the Wright heirs near the old mill and near the Wright Cemetery. Hance was short and liked to drink beverage alcohol. He married Sis Joyner and had children. Hance was a builder and built many of the bigger houses in the area including one for his sister Balzura. Hance was known as the brick man too. He had his own kiln; mixing and cooking his own bricks.

Several of the area folks went to Georgia to work in timber and tar. Hance carried his family there and they lived at a boarding house. It was reported that Hance got mad because Sis was friendlier with the other boarders than with him. He decided to walk home to Tabor, N.C. He walked the railroad track. Once he was on a long trestle crossing a wide river and he heard the train coming. He held himself by his arms down under the trestle until the train passed.

When he finally got to Tabor City around the year 1900, he was worn out and so were his shoes. He was starving and had only ten cents in his pocket. Should he buy food or a chew of tobacco? He chose tobacco since he would soon be to sister Balzura's house and she always had big pots of food cooked. When he got to Balzura's house, she was busy weaving on the loom, and did not set him a plate. He decided to walk on down to his sister Lizzie Boswell's house. Sister Lizzie did not have time to set him a plate either, she was delivering a new son that she named English Devon.

Hance became a bachelor and lived in a little house on his farm near his sister Lizzie. He built houses and chimneys and still liked to drink whiskey. One day a huge storm came up and blew his papers out the door. A few days later, someone found his land deed in a tree and carried it to Lizzie. She gave the deed to her oldest grandson. This made a neighbor angry. He was the husband of Lizzie's niece Effie. He took Lizzie to court about it, but she won. Hance's children grew up in the Piedmont area of North Carolina and one son Lennon ran a store at Warrenton, N.C. Many years later, genealogist Williard Wright found some of Hance's descendants. Many have visited cousins in Tabor City, and in 2007, a grandson Lucian Dow Wright of Conway, brought a small marker to Hance's grave in the old Wright Cemetery.

Alfred S. Fowler

As told by Ellen Watts Blanton and others.

Alfred S. Fowler was the son of James G. "Jim", and Edith Fowler and lived in the community called Fowler Town, straddling the N.C./S.C. border east of Tabor City. Alfred married first Mary Ann Watts, daughter of Eli, Sr. and Viney Ann Hinson Watts. They had several children. Alfred then married Lydia Fowler after Mary Ann died.

Alfred had the reputation for stealing. People could not leave things out. People in the fields hoeing, would take their hoes home at dinner time so they would not get stolen. Most people were farmers in America then. They helped at house and barn raisings and they branded their stock. One day a group of neighbors had been helping Alfred to raise a barn. They ate a delicious dinner, and were resting under the shade trees, when dog drug up a head of a sheep. One neighbor saw his brand on the sheep head and yelled," Well, damn it; we just had my sheep for dinner!"

The Stingiest Man in Mollie

Submitted by Richard Wright

The Reverend George Calvin Smith, a native of the Mollie Community, related a story about the stingiest man in Mollie in a sermon at St. Paul United Methodist Church in Tabor City, on November 11, 2007, as he was substituting for his son, the Reverend Dr. Jerome Smith, Pastor. Reverend Smith stated that this un-named gentleman from Mollie, who resided there many, many years ago, was so stingy that he would always un-harness his mule on the shady side of the barn. The man's reasoning was that if he un-harnessed his mule on the sunny side of the barn, that the shadow of the mule might want an ear of corn!

Reverend Smith said that the neighbors in the community often teased the man about all of his money and about how stingy he was. He was known for wearing the same pair of overalls and he had a noticeable hole in the left rear pocket. One time a bunch of the men in the community, gathered at the local country store, were teasing him about wearing out his back pocket because of all the money that he kept in it.

The stingiest man in Mollie then told them that he had worn a hole in the back pocket because he carried around, in that pocket, the dentures of his wife so that she would not eat between meals.

"The Picture Man"

-- Betty W. Hedgepath

Mr. Dewey Walker of Whiteville, NC, was known throughout Columbus County and surrounding counties as "the Picture Man". He owned one of the early Kodak cameras, and about 1925 he starting traveling from place to place taking pictures of individuals, families and pets. He also framed diplomas, made decorative marriage certificates, and death records. He framed and sold enlargements of pictures that he had hand-painted by professional artists. These were particularly desired by parents who had family members in the military during World War II. Many of these pictures can still be seen in local homes.

Born April 18, 1898, Dewey Walker was one of eighteen children born to William George Walker and his three wives. He married Emily Manning of Lebanon, NC, at age 32, and had two daughters: Hilda Grey Walker and Betty Rose Walker. He believed in God and attended several churches during his lifetime, the last being Whiteville United Methodist Church. He had the unique experience of being baptized with water from the River Jordan. He died November 11, 1982, at the age of 84 and is buried with his wife in the Lebanon Methodist Church Cemetery.

Dewey Walker is remembered with love and affection not only by his family but by his customers. His career spanned over fifty years and touched the lives of thousands of North Carolinians.

Skipper Compound Doesn't Work

--Slade Skipper

Years ago, before the days of refrigeration, most families preserved their meat and stored it in smokehouses. One problem was that small insects, called skippers, would get into the meat and cause it to spoil. Companies developed an additive called Skipper Compound, to control the infestation of skippers. This compound was often sold by traveling salesmen. On one occasion a traveling salesman was trying to sell some Skipper Compound to my grandfather. He assured him that the compound would keep the skippers out of his meat. My grandfather demurred, but the salesman kept insisting. Finally my grandfather said, "I have a whole bunch of Skippers up at my house. And nothing will keep those Skippers out of my meat!" My grandfather was named Lloyd Skipper.

Russell Z. Bailey, Union Soldier

Russell Z. Bailey was born 27 Jul 1938 in Bedford, Ohio. He enlisted in Illinois and was in the Union Army from 1861 to 1864. In 1865, he married his 1st wife, Cornelia Robinson, born 4 Feb 1845 in Harmony, New York. They moved from Illinois to Floyd County, Iowa. Their children were Loey Robinson Bailey, born Sep 1866 (Iowa); Elroy Byron Bailey; Leon A. Bailey, born 17 Jun 1874 (Iowa); and Earl Russell Bailey, born 25 Aug 1879 (Iowa). Cornelia died 21 Dec 1910 and is buried in the Chadbourn Memorial Cemetery. On 11 Nov 1912, Russell married Rena Duncan in Columbus County. Russell died 2 Feb 1918 in Columbus County.

The Wood Box

-- Ruth King, Chadbourn

My mother's Aunt Alice and Uncle Theodore Rivenbark lived in the Burgaw area of Pender County with their son, Crowell. At that time (in the 1930's), all of the cooking for the family was done on a wood stove. It was the task of the men in the family to see that the wood box was filled for the cook stove each day.

One morning, Uncle Theodore and Crowell were up early to go deer hunting. Aunt Alice reminded them that they needed to fill the wood box before leaving. After they left the kitchen, she was clearing the breakfast dishes. As she turned from the table and glanced out the window, she saw them walking off in the distance, heading for the woods, with the wood box still as empty as before!

Aunt Alice went on with her daily chores, her anger growing as she worked. They would expect supper that night as usual, but they expected her to fill the wood box herself in addition to doing all the cooking? Just then, she got an idea for a way to teach them a good lesson.

When Uncle Theodore and Crowell came in that night, tired and hungry from a long day of hunting, they entered the kitchen to find a wonderful meal, fully prepared, sitting on the table. The only problem was, all of the food was still raw! Uncle Theodore bellowed, "What's this? Why is this food not cooked?" Aunt Alice calmly replied from her rocking chair in the living room, "Is there any wood in the wood box?"

Needless to say, Aunt Alice never again had to remind the men to fill the wood box before leaving the house for the day.

The Junkman Comes on a Tuesday

--Rita Diane Stevens Jones

The year was 1954. Daddy was stationed in the Marshall Islands. This time the Army had not allowed me and Mama to hook up our little house trailer and follow Daddy, as we almost always did, when The Pentagon changed our address. Maybe it was because our trailer home wasn't seaworthy and not able to float to a small group of islands in the Pacific Ocean. More than likely, we couldn't go with Daddy because the military was busy testing the hydrogen bomb there on those tiny islands so far away. However, I think Daddy was joking when he said Mama and I couldn't go because the United States Army had heard too many stories about his mischievous daughter to allow her off the continental United States. Consequently, Mama and I left Glen Burnie, Maryland for the farm in Tabor City, North Carolina, and Grandma and Grandpa, Charlie Marshall Cox and Tempie Jane Norris Cox.

My Grandfather Cox was not only a hardworking farmer, but also an entrepreneur. He loved the land and raised fine tobacco. He was also a carpenter, and what we would call today, a real estate agent. He built, bought and sold land, farms, and homes. My grandparents also ran their own little country store, The C. M. Cox Store. The store was nestled between the homes of my great-grandmother, Martha Lucinda Faulk Norris, who had left her home in Sandy Plain when Great-Grandfather Norris died. That was so she could live near her youngest daughter, my Grandmother Tempie. Grandma Matt had died in 1946, so the house was rented. On the other side of the store sat the corncrib, two tobacco barns, a mule stable, and a pack house. The C. M. Cox Store was a popular gathering place for all the locals. All the smart politicians made sure to stop in often especially during election season.

Most days it fell to Grandma Tempie to work the garden, fix the big noon meal for the farmhands, and to tend the store. I was constantly underfoot and soon realized that the Pepsi Cola man and the Coca Cola man came on Monday. I was always sorry that the drink men managed not to meet at the store at the same time. I eagerly anticipated a wonderful brawl when one learned that his cola hadn't been the best seller the previous week. That much longed for event never happened. Nevertheless, I always managed rather loudly, because I thought both had to be deaf because neither seemed to hear me, to tell one and then the other the count from the previous week's competition. The cracker man had his day along with the bread man, the dry goods man and so on. The iceman learned quickly enough to check the back of his truck before leaving the C.M. Cox Store. It only took him a time or two of being forced to turn around at his next stop to return this little girl, he surely detested, who he would find, sitting among his big blocks of ice chipping away with his ice pick happily crunching. I didn't ride much in the ice truck after being discovered. But even so, I always managed to climb into that big old truck on iceman day for a big cold chunk of delicious ice.

The junkman, however, did not come to the store every week. I became especially interested in the junkman's schedule because, unlike the others, he didn't deliver. He picked up. And when he did, he put money in the hands of my grandma. I was constantly asking, "Grandma, when does the junkman come?" She always answered, "When he comes, it'll be on a Tuesday." I peppered her with questions until I learned that the junkman paid for anything made of metal. I honestly don't remember being told that only old useless stuff was sold to the junkman. I was too busy concentrating on the dollar signs registering in my nine year old head.

As fate would have it, one Tuesday the junkman arrived with his clanging goods dancing around in his now familiar rig which consisted of a worn out pickup with a rickety trailer lagging behind. On this particular Tuesday, Grandpa was in town on business; Grandma in the garden; Mama at the stove across the street in the big house, and Dinah Lu "tending store." My grandparents always called me Dinah Lu. I had been instructed to run across the dirt road to fetch Mama should a patron or deliveryman arrive. To my thinking, the junkman fell into neither of these categories. I felt not one twinge of conscience. But, I had been waiting for that man a long time. I had also been busy for many a day building my stash of metal goods behind the corncrib.

Grandma had many pots and pans. She hadn't even noticed the several iron skillets missing from the kitchen, various cooking utensils, and her new plug in sewing machine. Grandpa hadn't noticed that most of the mule tack, horseshoes, several tire rims, a variety of farm implements light enough for me to drag or carry, gas cans, tractor parts, stored tools, cans of nails and several other miscellaneous items were no longer in the correct place. Crime wasn't much of an issue back then on the farm. People assumed that when an item was put away, it would remain in its place until needed. Never again would they assume anything after that day.

The junkman and I exchanged greetings before he asked for Temp or Mart, my grandparents. He never asked for Mama. I told him they were on business, and I had been left in charge of the store. I also explained to him that we had quite a pile of junk that needed removing. The junkman and I ambled over behind the corncrib. I watched him intently as he surveyed the metal treasure mound I had so carefully erected. His expression never changed as I stood anxiously gazing up at him. The junkman said not a word until he gave me his best price, which I accepted gleefully. He even allowed me to sit in the back of the pickup as he skillfully backed behind the corncrib. I politely helped him load his newly purchased wares. Then he paid me. Impatiently I watched the junkman drive away slowly hauling away a much heavier load than when he had arrived. The moment he was out of sight, I scurried to my log playhouse my grandfather had built for me. There is where I kept squirreled away my bank, a big red Louisanne Coffee can. I was delighted as I lifted the can up and down to feel how much heavier it was. And now I had some green dollar bills, too.

I don't remember exactly when Grandpa and Grandma began missing things. I do remember conversations about missing items becoming more and more frequent over breakfasts of hot homemade biscuits and fresh peaches. I can remember becoming more and more uncomfortable during these conversations but not uncomfortable enough to confess any knowledge of the missing stuff. That is until one day a man, I barely recognized as my beloved grandpa, came stamping into the store door enraged and threatening to call the law.

"Somebody's going to the chain gang," he bellowed, "lest I get to 'um first." "They ain't a nail left on the place much less a hammer to nail 'em with."

"Well, Mart," Grandma said calmly, "since you're goin' after the law, you may as well tell 'um that my new Singer is missin' too."

With that news, Grandpa kicked the screen door right off its hinges.

"Well, that dang well does it," he exploded grabbing the truck keys off the rusty nail over the Pepsi box. "I'll be back with the sheriff directly."

Now I was quite familiar with the chain gang. Every now and then a big gray bus would pull off the road near the store. Men with guns stood watch as prisoners wearing bold striped black and white suits, chained together at the leg, disembarked. The prisoners were given sling blades, pulling their chains along, and as the guards watched eagle eyed; they cleaned the ditches on both sides of the road from daylight till dusk. At some time after hearing the name chain gang during Grandpa's tirade, I had sought refuge behind Grandma's ladder back chair. My grandma kept right on shelling those beans as I leaned forward to whisper in her ear that the junkman probably had the Singer.

"Hold on a minute, Mart," she said in her usual calm voice. "Dinah Lu has a good idea where the Singer went, and I 'magine where your tools will likely be fount, too."

My mother was summoned, and after a prolonged interrogation, she promised me a spanking I would never forget. To my relief my grandparents intervened. There would be no spanking. Instead I was sent to fetch my precious Louisanne can and give it to Grandpa. I had rather have had the spanking, but for once, kept my mouth shut. Carrying my Louisanne can by the wire handle, Grandpa went off to find the junkman.

From the whispered conversations when Grandpa returned with most of our possessions, which he had paid twice the price to retrieve, I still don't think the junkman had fared as well as I had. I never saw that junkman again.

A long time passed before I asked my Grandma about the junkman. Grandma calmly stopped kneading her biscuit dough, turned to look at me standing on a stool beside her, and said quietly, "Dinah Lu, the junkman won't be comin' on a Tuesday ever again."

HISTORICAL PERSPECTIVES

Mill Branch Primitive Baptist Church

Submitted by Richard Wright

Mill Branch Primitive Baptist Church, chartered by the Wright, Harrelson, and other local families in 1855 continues to have services to this day. The church, located on Peacock Road, known as the Whiteville-Conwayborough Road, at the intersection with Mill Branch Church Road and Minos Meares Road, originally was a one-story wooden structure with high ceilings. At the entrance were two doors, with one being for the men to enter the church and the other for the ladies. Down the center of the church were columns from a point between the two front doors going down the center of the church almost to the pulpit. There was a banister connecting each column.

The pine pews faced the pulpit with a row being on each side of the columns. On the men's side of the church were several shorter pews which were placed perpendicular to the other pews. These were for the male members of the church to sit so that they were at the right hand of the preacher and facing the right side of him. On the left of the preacher were some shorter pews for the female members of the church to use.

Services were held at Mill Branch Primitive Baptist Church on the first Sunday of each month and on the Saturday proceeding the first Sunday. The members usually started arriving around 10:00 o'clock, in the morning, to visit and about 10:30 would begin going inside to sing hymns acappella using a hymn book which was written like a book of poetry and which contained old familiar hymns with no musical notes.

There was no musical instrument in the church and there was always a song leader who started out with the first verse and after he or she sang about one line of the hymn, everyone else would join in. My recollection from my childhood is that each hymn basically sounded like *Amazing Grace*!

People would continue to gather during the period of the singing of the hymns and about 11:00 o'clock a.m. the pastor of the Church would welcome everyone, and an official opening hymn would be announced.

After that hymn, there would be an opening prayer that lasted several minutes. I recall that each of those in attendance would place his or her head, during the prayer, on the back of the pew in front. After the opening prayer there would be another hymn and the pastor would then invite visiting preachers to speak. Often there were three or four visiting preachers and sometimes the service would last for 2 hours or more.

The preachers did not prepare a sermon and would preach only if divinely inspired; however, it seems like that at each service just about all of the preachers did find the divine inspiration to preach at some length!

Never was an offering plate passed and there was no Sunday School and no Church budget. The minister was not paid and usually had some occupation such as store owner, carpenter, farmer, or some other vocation or trade which the preacher used to support his family and himself.

Each Church in the Mill Branch Primitive Baptist Association had its own Sunday service, with another service on the preceding Saturday. The members of Mill Branch would often go to Tabor Primitive Baptist Church, Simpson Creek Primitive Baptist Church, Pireway Primitive Baptist Church, Black Creek Primitive Baptist Church or some other Primitive Baptist Church on the other Sundays.

Each November there was a three-day association which would be attended by many, many preachers from all over North and South Carolina and many, many people. Preaching would last most of the day on Friday, Saturday and Sunday and there would be abundant food served at lunch time on tables outside of the church. I can remember men preparing hot coffee in huge iron kettles set over an open fire in the church yard.

By the time I was old enough to remember going there for services with my dad the first Sunday of each month, the old Mill Branch School was gone; however, I do remember there was a nice outhouse for the men and another nice outhouse for the ladies.

My Grandmother, Lillon Ward Wright, born in 1877, joined Mill Branch Church in 1890. She remained a member until her death in 1973, a total of 83 years. She considered herself a failure as a hostess if she did not accommodate at least 20 extra people at her home during the November Association.

The Charleston Earthquake of 1886

Submitted by Richard Wright

The Charleston Earthquake of 1886 caused the biggest jolt throughout the southeastern United States in recorded history. The big jolt came at 9:50 on the evening of Tuesday, August 31, 1886 and lasted about 1 minute. Much damage was caused in Charleston and reports indicate that over 2,000 buildings were damaged and that between 60 and 110 lives were lost.

My grandmother was Lillon Ward Wright, born 26 November, 1877 and died 14th November, 1973. She was 8 years old at that time, and residing with her parents John William Ward and Anzaline Harrelson Ward, and some younger siblings on a farm between Vinegar Hill, Black Creek School, and Mill Branch Primitive Baptist Church. It was located on the south side of Richard Wright Road, near the intersection with Mill Branch Church Road, just north of the run of Grissett Swamp. (This home was later purchased by Maloy Wright, the brother of Lillon Ward's husband, Mayon Wright, whom she married in 1898.)

She related to me many times about the day that she and her family were preparing for bed on a hot August evening in 1886 when the ground started shaking, and items began falling out of corner cupboards, cabinets and other locations. The farm animals became very agitated, and cracks appeared in the plaster of the old home. Her father collected the family around him and began reading from the Bible in an effort to keep everyone calm. At that time the railroad was being laid between Chadbourn and Conway and the piles of rails, ready to be placed on the ties, were stacked along the right-of-way in Mt. Tabor just about 3 miles west from the farm. My grandmother remembered that during that period when the earth was shaking, she and her family could hear the railroad rails clanging together as the piles were jolted by the magnitude

Wikipedia reports that structural damage of the Great Charleston Earthquake of 1886.was reported several hundred miles from Charleston. It was felt as far north as Boston, as far west as New Orleans, as far south as Cuba and as far east as Bermuda. It is reported that it was between 6.6 and 7.3 on the Richter scale. There is still minor earthquake activity today which takes place in the Charleston area, and that these might be a continuation of aftershocks of that Great Charleston Earthquake of 1886.

Toys and Games

--Betty W. Branch

As I travel around I am overwhelmed with all the plastic "toys" that litter the yards of the homes that are blessed with children. Toys and games have really changed since I was a child. The only tractor that I knew about was a gigantic "Oliver" that belonged to my dad and a Farmall M tractor with spiked wheels that was used at my uncle's sawmill. We had no John Deere tractors but now John Deere emblems are on everything from clothing, linens, dishes, toys, jewelry and anything else you can mention. Porcelain dolls were a must for every little girl. They didn't do things like talking, burping, wetting, walking, or even crying. They were hard and cold but loved by their owner. One of my favorite places to play was under my grandmother's house. Yes, under it. Houses were built high off the ground at that time for ventilation, I suppose, and there was no under-pinning;. Anyway, we would crawl under the house and play with our doll, catch doodlebugs, and do anything else our minds would lead us to do. One day while playing under the house, I laid my beautiful tiny porcelain doll on the large floor joists as I played around. When Mom called, I crawled out and left my doll. Days later when I thought about her, she could not be found. How I wish I had her now.

I mentioned catching doodlebugs. If you don't know what a doodlebug is, oh yes, they are still around, I will tell you. Their biological name is Antlions, which I did not know until the computer age. They are usually found under a shelter in dry soil. We would take a twig or string and dangle it in their conical hole, trying to coax them out, as we chanted, "Doodlebug, Doodlebug, your house is on fire."

Since we were around the tobacco barns so much in the summer, the younger boys would take a tobacco stick; tie some tobacco twine around one end, leaving a long string for a line, and climb aboard the finest horse in the neighborhood. In their imagination the horse could be a black stallion, chestnut brown, silver, white, or Palomino, it was up to the rider, as they raced back and forth in the dry sandy farm road.

Don't forget about making toad frog houses. When we found a little moist dirt we would pile it around our bare foot (no child wore shoes in the summer) and pack it down, really hard. As soon as the dirt was firm, we would carefully slip our foot out so it would not cave in, leaving an opening for frogs to enter. I don't remember ever seeing a frog inside one but in our imagination.

On weekends all the families would gather together for rest and to discuss the happenings in the community and on the farm. After a hearty meal prepared by the women, the men would sit on the front porch in the rocking chairs and smoke their pipes, cigars, and cigarettes. Lighters were not available then so they "lit up" with kitchen matches, that were big and used to light fires in the stove, and "penny" matches which were smaller and a box only cost one cent. When they blew out the match, they would toss it out into the yard. No problem, the yards were bare and Mom saw that they were "swept" clean with a "brush" broom each Saturday. We children would pick up the match stems and make farm roads, barns and fences with them. We spent hours on our knees, designing our masterpieces. Ignored by the men folk, we encouraged smoking! It gave us more matches, thus longer fences and bigger barns.

What about those slingshots that the boys crafted! A forked limb off a tree and a strip of rubber bicycle tubing made a deadly weapon for birds. The birds had to fly fast or they would be on the "supper" table that night. Moms were not afraid for the boys to take their slingshot and walk in the woods or around the farm. There was no fear of kidnapping, stalking, molesting or any of the things that plague us today. They were told to watch for snakes and be home for supper and chores.

We also enjoyed a cool dip in the pond or little creek on the farm. We didn't know anything about "bikinis" or "thongs," just "come in as you are." We rolled old tires around, no speed limits. We made dolls and spinning tops from wooden spools after Mom had used all the thread for sewing our clothes and making beautiful quilts to keep us warm at night since there was no heat in the house. I remember when Mom and her sisters would gather to make a quilt; my girl cousins and I would play under the quilt and listen to the ladies "discuss "the community affairs. No boys were allowed; this was strictly a "hen" party.

Yes, the games children play have really changed, for better or worse, who knows? But it was a lot of fun to run and play with siblings and cousins and then crawl in bed, exhausted from a wonderful day of physical activity; ready to dream about tomorrow. Do children experience this feeling today as they stay inside, playing games alone, in silence? Who knows?

Cemetery "Workings" and Other Musings

--Dixie Wilson Rogers

The title of this little story, as you will see, in no way sufficiently documents the annual, and sometimes more often, event – the cemetery "working" or "cleaning".

With the advent of the motor driven lawn mower, the leaf blowers and mulchers, coupled with the busy life-styles we have adopted, this has become a fading event. What a shame!

Cemetery cleanings for many, many years were necessary traditional neighborhood social events. However, as social as it was, there was no need for anyone to buy a new hat or wear their Sunday shoes, get out their linen napkins or plan for refreshments. No money was spent on invitations, stamps, printed tee shirts, etc. It was most often a fall happening and usually a first frost would cause someone to remark, "the cemetery needs cleaning" and the word would get around. Any day would do for, as I have said, life was not so hectic and, too, this was an important event, not to be missed.

Preparation was minimum, to say the least. Just take the rake, and maybe an extra one if you have one, clippers in case something needs trimming back and gloves for any tender palms. Of course, don't forget your hat.

What a wonderful opportunity to honor and remember one's ancestors. Of course, you didn't (or don't) just work around your own family's graves; everyone started on one side of the cemetery and worked to the other side. This gave all an opportunity to remember one another's families and hear their stories.

When I lived in Columbus County and could hear about the workings down at Pierce Cemetery, I always arranged to be there and participate. My maternal grandparents and a beloved maternal aunt were buried there and I was familiar with most of the names on the other tombstones, so I felt it my duty, and my pleasure, to be present

I vividly remember one of those fall afternoons among the tombstones, leaves, twigs and friends. We worked hard all afternoon and left the cemetery looking freshly raked and noticeably cared for. (The cemetery, not us). That particular afternoon I happened to rake next to Miss Frances Pierce, a maiden lady who lived within walking distance of the cemetery, probably where she had lived her entire life. My, for an 80-year-old, she could really rake and, at about 35, it took some concentration on my part to keep up with her. When I got home that afternoon, I must have looked rather bedraggled, for when George saw me, he asked, "What is wrong with you?" and, without hesitation, I exclaimed, "I've been raking next to an 80-year-old all afternoon and I am TIRED!"

Now, I will digress with some other musings I have on my mind about the care and upkeep of cemeteries. My friend, Mary Currie Sears, told me she remembered how her Mother was known as the official overseer of the cemeteries in her little town of Parkton. Mrs. Currie, whose husband was a successful physician and landowner, always had at her disposal, a "yard man" who could assist her. She kept up with the condition of the area cemeteries and, when they needed attention, she knew who in the community had ties to that particular graveyard and could be called on to help. She provided the supervision, encouragement and some financial help when necessary. Mary often wondered how the cemeteries were kept after her parents died and her family left the area. How long did Mrs. Currie's legacy continue?

Another angle to my cemetery experiences is the abuse tombstones get from modern lawn mowers and other equipment. Go to a cemetery and look at the toppled stones - hit by a lawn mower, most probably. I came upon George's paternal Grandfather's broken stone, which had been there since 1927 in the Hawfield's Cemetery but had obviously not fallen over, broken as it was, by itself. I called a monument company to be told the fee would be $100 to go out there plus whatever repair work had to be done. A bit pricey for me so I hurried off to the hardware store and spent quite a bit of time reading glue labels. Finally, "Guerilla Glue" was chosen (I am not being paid to advertise their product). I was now ready to set my plan into action. It was an easy decision for me to make, to "do it yourself". What was not so easy was to convince George that he could be the laborer and I the supervisor. Well, it happened and I was so proud. $4.95, plus tax, and a little gas to get there were the expenditures. That was about ten years ago and, when we are now in that neighborhood, we check it out. The tombstone repair is holding up beautifully.

Graveyards are full of our history and have many stories to tell. I even know a few more but for now, if you hear of a neighborhood cemetery cleaning, let me know - I'll try to get there.

Chadbourn Berry Growers

S. Carroll Pearsall, Riegelwood, NC

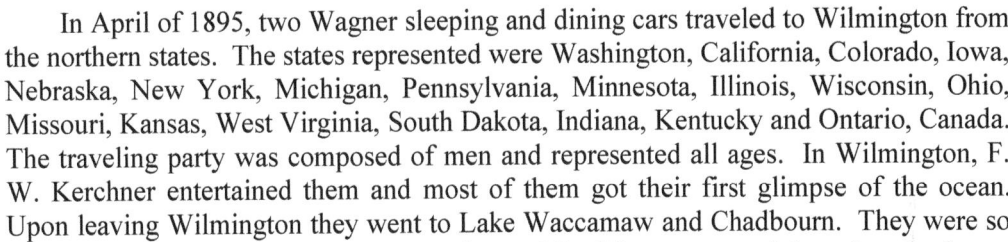

In April of 1895, two Wagner sleeping and dining cars traveled to Wilmington from the northern states. The states represented were Washington, California, Colorado, Iowa, Nebraska, New York, Michigan, Pennsylvania, Minnesota, Illinois, Wisconsin, Ohio, Missouri, Kansas, West Virginia, South Dakota, Indiana, Kentucky and Ontario, Canada. The traveling party was composed of men and represented all ages. In Wilmington, F. W. Kerchner entertained them and most of them got their first glimpse of the ocean. Upon leaving Wilmington they went to Lake Waccamaw and Chadbourn. They were so impressed with the latter that they bought twenty-seven town lots, while fifty or more of them bought farms. Most of the fruit growers were members of the original Sunny South Colony.

There was plenty of good land. Joseph A. Brown and his brother, R. E. Lee Brown had purchased cut over timberland. Advertisement of land and opportunities were published in northern papers. A typical advertisement in the *Minneapolis Journal* on December 12, 1896 reads as follows:

"15,000 ACRES splendid farm lands for sale on easy terms in subdivisions, from: 10 acres up; prices ranging between $6 and $15 per acre; located near Chadbourn, N. C., adjoining the Sunny South Colony, where already over 50 Western families are located. Two railroad stations on the land. Healthy climate, no chills or malaria; good water; no drought; best place in the world for winter gardening, fruit and cattle raising; only 20 hours rail from New York; cheap freights; two and three crops raised on same land in one year; 40 acres constitutes a big farm; semi-monthly excursions. For map, particulars sic; address Doc Mercer, Chadbourn, N. C., or No. 270, N. 3d St., St. Paul, Minn."

A Chadbourn Excursion advertisement was also placed in the *Farm, Field and Fireside*, of Chicago, Ill., on 11 Sep 1897.

It would be impossible to cover all the families that relocated to Chadbourn. From the Chadbourn census records, these names were abstracted as those listed as fruit growers. The states in parentheses were the state of birth. Some family history is provided from the census and other sources. They include the following:

1. James A. Allen, b abt.1853 (Illinois); wife Ida Allen b abt.1856 (Illinois). Daughter, Elva M. Allen, b Oct 1877 (Illinois) married Robert M. Newland in Columbus County; son, Charles A. Allen b Jun 1880 (Illinois); daughter, Cora M. Allen b Dec 1881 (Missouri); son, Henry Allen b Jan 1884 (Missouri); daughter, Anna C. Allen, b Feb 1886 (Missouri); son, Wilbur A. Allen, b Jun 1889 (Illinois); son, George E. Allen, b May 1894 (Illinois); daughter, Helen B. Allen, born Dec 1895 (Illinois).
2. Elroy Byron Bailey b abt. 1872 (Iowa), son of Russell Z. Bailey; wife, Myrtle A. Clark b abt. 1874 (Iowa). Elroy was a native of Marble Rock, Iowa and came to Chadbourn in the fall of 1898. He died 19 Apr 1948. Myrtle died at her home in Chadbourn on 14 Apr 1962. Elroy and Myrtle were members of the Chadbourn Baptist Church. Both are buried in the Chadbourn Memorial Cemetery. Three sons: Guy Loey Bailey, born abt. 1895 (Iowa) married Oprah Koonce on 8 Oct 1919 in Columbus County; Clare Russell Bailey b abt. 1893 (Iowa), married Elizabeth E. Smith on 25 Dec 1916 in Columbus County; and Wayne Elroy Bailey b 21 Nov 1899, Columbus County, married Myrtle M. Jolly on 21 Sep 1921 in Columbus County. Wayne married 2nd Mrs. Dorothy Elliot on 21 Feb 1960 in Columbus County.

3. Russell Z. Bailey, born 27 Jul 1938, Bedford, Ohio. He enlisted in Illinois and was in the Union Army from 1861 to 1864. In 1865, he married his 1st wife, Cornelia Robinson, born 4 Feb 1845 in Harmony, New York. They moved from Illinois to Floyd County, Iowa. Cornelia died 21 Dec 1910 and is buried in the Chadbourn Memorial Cemetery. On 11 Nov 1912, Russell married Rena Duncan in Columbus County. Russell died 2 Feb 1918 in Columbus County. The children were: Loey Robinson Bailey born Sep 1866 (Iowa), Elroy Byron Bailey, Leon A. Bailey born 17 Jun 1874 (Iowa) and Earl Russell Bailey, born 25 Aug 1879 (Iowa).
4. John E. Barber, b abt.1863 (Ohio) partner with Chas W. Foster.
5. George Hemperley Boughner born 13 Sep 1875 (Pennsylvania) married Annie Baird, born 25 Nov 1875 in Clarks, Nebraska, at the home of M. M. Walker, Minister in Columbus County on 18 Dec 1896. Daughters, Leota Boughner, Fannie Boughner, Nellie J. Boughner, Ruth Boughner and Grace Elizabeth Boughner. Fannie married C. B. Crawford. Nellie J. married Earl W. Miller, Sr., in Columbus County on 9 Nov 1919. Ruth married Rubie Nye and died at Hill Haven Nursing Home in Wilmington on 17 May 1993. Ruth was a retired primary school teacher. Rubie Nye was born in Marion County, SC and died in Robeson County on 30 Nov 1968. They had one son William Baird Nye born in Columbus County. Grace Elizabeth and Leo Elvington were married on 15 Jun 1935 in Columbus County. Grace died in Dillon, SC on 19 February 1998. In Columbus County on 4 Oct 1921, Leota married Samuel Ernest Cain of Bladen County. George died in a Dillon, S. C. hospital on 22 Sep 1971. Annie died in Granville County, NC on 24 Sep 1958. George and Annie are buried in Chadbourn Memorial Cemetery.
6. Morton Peterson Casey, b abt.1856 (Michigan), wife Laura Casey, b abt.1871 (Illinois). Laura was a widow in 1910, living in Montgomery, Pa., with four children: Thomas Casey, Morton Casey, Viola Casey and Randel Casey.
7. John Chapin, b abt. 1853 (Canada), wife Emily A. Chapin, b abt. 1857 (Canada).
8. Chas L. Colburn, b abt.1837 (Vermont), wife Harriette Colburn, b abt.1837 (Vermont).
9. Alvin Foster Coultas, b abt.1870 (Illinois), wife Nora Coultas, b abt.1876 (Illinois). A daughter, Pauline Lois Coultas b 12 Nov 1899 in Columbus County. A daughter Marian Francis Coultas was born 16 Sep 1898 and married John Paul Robertson on 1 Sep 1920 in Columbus County. Marion died 30 Sep 1960 in Richmond County, N. C. In 1930, Nora is residing in Virden, Illinois with her son, Alvin Foster Coultas, Jr, who was born 5 Apr 1901 in Columbus County. Elizabeth Rebecca Coultas was born 20 Mar 1903 and married James R. Miller on 6 Sep 1920 in Columbus County. Gertrude Rush Coultas was born 7 Nov 1906. Catherine Lena Coultas was born 8 Mar 1910.
10. Frank E. Coultas, b abt.1871 (Illinois), (brother to Alvin Foster Coultas), wife Elizabeth Coultas, b abt.1877 (Illinois). In 1910 Frank and Elizabeth were in Virdon, Ill.
11. George Fea, b abt 1841 (Michigan), died 22 Feb 1924, near Chadbourn; wife Lydia Fea, b abt. 1846 (Michigan), died 12 Jan 1924, Columbus Co, NC. A daughter, Edna L. Fea married 18 Jan 1911 in Columbus County, NC, N. Boston Stephens. A daughter Fea, Mrs. James Gallagher resided in Iowa, Michigan.
12. Chas W. Foster, b abt.1860 (Pennsylvania), wife Nellie Foster, b abt. 1865 (Illinois).
13. George or Joseph Freedman b abt.1861 (Austria), wife Johanna Freedman b abt.1858 (Austria) died 28 May 1914, Columbus County. Children: John D. Freedman b 28 May 1886 in Colorado, George Washington Freedman born 28 Apr 1889 in Colorado, Joseph Freedman b 14 Mar 1894 in Denver, CO., Stephen Freedman b 18 Aug 1895 in Colorado; Mary (Mattie) Freedman b abt. 1898; Wilmer Freedman b abt 1905. In 1920, George Washington Freeman was residing in Portsmouth, VA. In 1920, Stephen Freedman was residing in Danville, VA. Wilmer Wade Freedman married Brightie Othello Stroud on 23 Jan 1930 in Columbus County and they had a son, Wilmer Brice Freedman. Wilmer and Brightie died in Whiteville.
14. Chas B. Goodrich b abt. 1875 (Illinois) married 26 Jul 1899, Columbus Co, NC; Florence L. Moors, b abt. 1873(Michigan).
15. Herman R. Goodrich, b abt.1835 (New York); wife Francie B., b abt.1841 (New York).
16. Albert Gonser was born 12 Sep 1856 in Dekalb County, Indiana. His wife was Charlotte, b abt.1861 (Iowa). In 1920, residing in Cross Creek, Cumberland Co, NC. Albert died 10 Mar 1934 in Fayetteville.
17. Benjamin Moran (Reginia) Hampton was born abt.1852 in Pennsylvania. His wife Mary Ann Morgan b abt.1853 (Pennsylvania). A son Benjamin Hampton b abt. 1880 in Colorado. In 1910 Benjamin is residing in Tularosa, New Mexico.

18. Benjamin Hoerner Harnly or Harnley b abt.1871 (Pennsylvania), wife Grace Louise Williams, b abt.1882 (Illinois). They were married in Columbus County on 8 Apr 1903. A son Harold Shepard Harnly was b abt.3 Sep 1905 in Columbus County. Ben and Grace were residing in Lakeland, Polk Co, Florida in 1930. In the household was a son, Benjamin E. born 1913 in Kansas and her dad, John E. Williams, b abt.1852 (New York). Benjamin was a veteran of WW11 and died in Alexandria, Virginia on 19 Feb 1996. Harold died in Huntsville, Alabama on 12 Jul 1998. Benjamin Hoerner Harnly died in Polk County, FL in Jan 1956. Grace died in Polk County, FL in May 1957.
19. Jessie S. Hamandz, b abt.1873 (Illinois), wife May b abt.1882, (Kansas).
20. G. E. Horton, b abt.1845 (New York), wife Martha, b abt.1847 (Illinois).
21. Jedediah V. (J. V.) Howe, b abt.1847 (New York), wife Harriette (Hattie) Linn b abt.1857 (New York), died 23 Apr 1902. She is buried in the Chadbourn Cemetery. A daughter, Bertha Howe born 6 Mar 1887 (Michigan), married William White Usher 8 Nov 1903 in Columbus County. William was born 23 May 1876 and died at Columbus County Hospital on 10 Mar 1957. Bertha Howe Usher died on 26 May 1962 in Rutherfordton, N. C. William and Bertha are buried in the Chadbourn Memorial Cemetery. There was another daughter, Zillah b abt 1892 (Michigan).
22. Elonzo R. Huse, b abt.1844 (New York), wife Martha b abt.1845 (Michigan). Daughters, Burnie Huse, b abt. 1873 (Michigan) and Beulah Huse, b abt. 1885 (Michigan).
23. Martin Francis Leonhart born 26 Dec 1841 (Germany) came to Columbus County from Iowa with second wife, Ida Louise, born 12 Dec 1856 (Germany). Martin immigrated to the U. S. in 1854. Martin's first wife was Agnes Rattray. He was a Union Veteran having served in Iowa. Martin died 20 Oct 1909. In 1920 Ida thought to be a widow residing with daughter Emma Panish in Titusville, Brevard Co, FL. Ida died in Titusville in 1933. A daughter Agnes married Rufus King Moors. A son Charles Rattray Leonhart was born 1872 (Iowa) and died in 1918.
24. Samuel T. Loman born 14 Mar 1860 (Virginia); wife Superia Agnes 12 Apr 1860 (Pennsylvania). A son, George Franklin Loman was born 20 Jan 1888 (Pennsylvania) and died 23 Jan 1920. George married Lee Thompson on 20 Jul 1913 in Columbus County. There were three daughters, all born Pennsylvania, Rachel Maria born 25 Jan 1891 died 20 Jul 1984 in Wilmington, never married; Eva Ruth b 10 Feb 1893 died 6 Feb 1968 in Wilmington, never married; Ada Lillian, 2 Feb 1895 died 10 Dec 1987 in Wilmington, never married. Samuel died in Wilmington on 14 Mar 1931. Superia died in Wilmington on 15 Dec 1930. Members of the Loman family are buried in the Chadbourn Memorial Cemetery.
25. Daniel M. Lufkin, b abt. 1844 (New Hampshire), wife Elizabeth b abt. 1847 (Ireland).
26. Byron Moors, b. abt 1835 (New York), wife Amanda A. Moors, b abt. 1837 (Delaware) parents of Rufus King Moors.
27. Rufus King Moors was born abt. 1865 in Greenville, Michigan, son of Byron W. Moors. At the age of 36, on 26 Jun 1901, Rufus married Agnes Leonhart, (Iowa) age 20, at the home of Martin Francis Leonhart in Columbus County. Two daughters, Amber Louise and Maude Eula Moors. Amber Louise Moors was born 21 May 1902, married Evans Sanford Hand born 5 Feb 1897, on 15 Feb 1921 in Columbus County. Amber died in Asheville on 8 Dec 1990. Evans Sanford Hand died 15 Mar 1972. Evans and Amber are buried in the Chadbourn Memorial Cemetery. Maude Eula Moors was born 14 Jun 1905 in Columbus County. Maude married Alfred B. Brady, Sr. Maude died on 20 Dec 1985 in Brooks County, Ga. Rufus King Moors died 4 Jul 1953. Agnes Leonhart Moors died in Columbus County Hospital on 31 Oct 1966. Rufus and Agnes Moors were members of the Chadbourn Presbyterian Church and are buried in Chadbourn Memorial Cemetery.
28. James Tate Newland was born 25 March 1857 in Bedford, Indiana and died 4 Dec 1944 in Chadbourn. His first wife, Fannie Rosalia, born 11 Mar 1854 in Illinois, died 20 Feb 1905 and is buried in the Chadbourn Memorial Cemetery. James married second in Columbus County on 9 Oct 1907, Alice H. Brown, born 25 May 1865 (North Carolina), sister of James A. Brown. Alice died 19 Jul 1943. Child of 2nd marriage was Patience Brown Newland. By his first marriage, James had sons: Dr. Leroy Tate Newland born 7 Mar 1885, Galva, Iowa; resided in Charlotte, NC and Union Point, Ga., traveled to Korea as Foreign Missionary with the Presbyterian Church; Harry Taylor Newland born 16 Jan 1883, Galva, Iowa, married Margaret (Maggie) Lou Middleton, resided Wilmington; Robert Melvin Newland born 3 Mar 1800 in Ida County, Iowa, married Melva M. Allen in Columbus County on 14 Jul 1904, resided Doswell, Va., and Charles Benjamin Newland born Galva, Iowa, 23 Nov 1891, married Gertrude Hewitt on 21 Feb 1917 in Columbus County, resided in Chadbourn and Willard. Charles died

8 Sep 1944 and is buried in the Chadbourn Memorial Cemetery. A daughter, Estelle May Newland was born 9 Sep 1881 (Iowa) and married Henry Pittman on 28 Dec 1905 in Columbus County, resided Elizabethtown. Estelle died 26 May 1979 in Bladen County. James and Alice were members of the Chadbourn Presbyterian Church and are buried in the Chadbourn Memorial Cemetery.

29. Dodge Sweet Payne, b abt.1833 (New York), wife Elizabeth Allen Chillson, b abt. 1828 (Rhode Island). A daughter, Sarah M., b abt. 1862 (Nebraska). In 1920, Dodge S. Payne, a widower was living with daughter Hope Payne b abt. 1857 (Wisconsin) in Callahan, California. A grandson, Glenn W. Payne, b abt. 1891 (Iowa) was living with them in Callahan, CA.

30. Fred H. Payne, b abt.1858 (Illinois), wife Lizzie R. b abt.1866 (Missouri). A son of Dodge S. Payne.

31. Josiah (Joseph) Perrin, b abt.1856 (England), wife Fannie (Annie) b abt.1860 (England). Thought to be residing in Paw Paw, Michigan in the 1920 census. In 1930, couple was in Antwerp, Michigan.

32. Elwood A. Pifer was born 9 Mar 1854 in West Unity, Ohio. Elwood died 12 Jul 1938 at the Columbus County Hospital. His wife Mary E. Zigler was born 1 Jan 1857 in Rome, Ohio. Elwood and Mary came to Chadbourn from Oak Lake, Canada. Mary died on 1 Nov 1931. They are both buried in the Chadbourn Memorial Cemetery. Elwood and Mary were members of the Methodist Church in Chadbourn. Sons, Willis Pifer of Russell, Ky., Roy Pifer of Hadon Height, N. J., Somerton Pifer of Vancouver, B. C. and daughters; Mrs. Eva Trimble of Perkin, Ill., and Chillicothe, OH; Mrs. Clara Smith of Petersburg, Fla., aka Mrs. Arthur Smith of Chillicothe, OH, Mrs. Bertha Grassie of Philadelphia, aka Mrs. Bertha Andrews Springfield, Mass., and Mrs. Beryl Walker of Los Angeles, Calif., aka Mrs. Beryl Whitlow of Alton, Ill. A daughter, Mrs. James Byrd died before 1931.

33. Thomas Hadden Ramsbottom, b abt. 1857 (Missouri), wife Lena b. 1873 (Missouri). A daughter, Bernice b abt. 1894 ((Missouri) and a daughter Gladys b abt. 1901 in Columbus County. In 1920 the family was residing with family in Monroe, MO.

34. G. S. Reid, b abt 1862(Virginia), wife Celestia b abt. 1877 (Virginia).

35. Joseph S. Shaver, b abt.1854 (Ohio). Joseph was widowed by 1910. In 1920 residing in Hendersonville, NC with brother John Shaver and son Robert Shaver. John and Robert are single. J. S. Shaver was ran over by an automobile and instantly killed near Hendersonville on 7 Jun 1924. The accident was unavoidable.

36. John H. Shaver, b abt.1862 (Ohio), brother to Joseph S. Shaver.

37. T. A. Shaver, b abt.1841 (Ohio); wife Santa or Sinda L. b abt.1844 (Ohio). In 1910, she was a widow residing in Chadbourn with daughter, Ada b abt. 1881 (Ohio).

38. David Smithman, b abt.1861 (England), wife Stepan L., b abt.1867 (Canada). Sons were Ernest D. Smithman b abt. 1887 (North Carolina) who died on 10 Apr 1971 in Fayetteville; and Herbert b abt. 1890 (North Carolina). Daughters, Elsie L., b abt. 1893 (North Carolina); Mabel A., b abt 1894 (North Carolina); Lucy G., b abt. 1896 South Dakota; Mary H., b abt. 1898 South Dakota.

39. Samuel E. Trask, b abt. 1858 (Illinois); wife Nettie M., b abt. 1869 (Illinois). Sons, Roy Edmund Trask b 30 Oct 1892 (Illinois); Joseph H. b abt. 1898 (Illinois), Louise I. Trask, b abt. 1907 (Illinois). In 1910, this family is residing in Chicago, Ill.

40. Frank Wesley, b abt.1855 (France), wife Mary b abt.1861 (Bohemia). Daughters, Louetta b 1884 (Colorado); Josephine b 1887 (Colorado); son John Deming Wesley b 5 Apr 1890 (Colorado); son Joseph Patrick Wesley b 25 Sep 1891 (Colorado), daughter Mary b 1894 (Colorado); Irene b 1896 (North Carolina); son Edward b 1899 (North Carolina).

41. Charles White b abt.1875 (Canada), brother to John White

42. John White b abt.1871 (Canada), brother to Charles White.

43. James E. Whitener b abt.1864 (Massachusetts), wife Emma b abt.1869 (Illinois). Sons, John I. Whitener, b Jul 1893 (Illinois); James S. Whitener, b Jan 1897 (North Carolina).

44. Harvey Wayne Whitney born 13 Dec 1847 (Ohio), died 9 Oct 1922, Columbus Co, NC; wife Lucy Ann Tooley b 2 Sep 1859 (Illinois) died 28 Apr 1916 in Chadbourn. A son, Cornelius was born 15 Mar 1894 and died 14 Oct 1919, buried Chadbourn Memorial Cemetery. A daughter, Lottie Whitney b 8 Aug 1903 in Columbus County, married William Edward Covil. Lottie died 15 Feb 1973 in Wilmington. Harvey and Lucy are buried in the Chadbourn Memorial Cemetery.

45. Herman J. Wilson, b abt.1832 (Ohio), wife Alice b abt.1856 (New York).

By 1905 according to newspaper accounts, there were huge berry loses as a result of a lack of railroad cars and scheduling. Some of the berry growers took to growing other crops. The 1910 census reflects that occupations were no longer listed as "Fruit Grower", and the designation had been replaced with "Farmer". The Daniel F. Strole family was living in Lamard, Wayne County, Indiana in 1900. According to *Chadbourn and Her Sunny South Colony* by Glenn F. Strole, the Strole family did not come to Chadbourn until 1907. Glenn Franklin Strole was born 3 May 1893 in (Illinois) married Inez Wilkes on 30 Jun 1920 in Columbus County. She was born 12 Jul 1894 and was a native of Chester Hill, OH. Children were: John Philip Strole of Chadbourn; daughters, Jean Elizabeth Strole who married Richardson Edward Holland, Jr., and Rachel Estelle Strole married Arnette Matthews. Glenn died 24 Mar 1966. Inez died 2 Nov 1979. Glenn and Inez were members of the Chadbourn Baptist Church and are buried in Chadbourn Memorial Cemetery.

In 1910, Alvin Coultas' occupation was listed as Real Estate, Jedediah V. Howe listed as a Proprietor, Harvey Whitney was listed as a mail server and Thomas H. Ramsbottom was listed as Postmaster. The following families listed in the 1900 census were not found in the 1910 census of Chadbourn: Allen, Barber, Casey, Chapin, Colburn, F. E. Coultas, Foster, Charles & Herman Goodrich, Hampton, Hamandz, Huse, Lufkin, Perrin, Reid, John Shaver, Smithman, Trask, Charles and John White, Whitener, and Wilson.

Corrections to *Columbus County, North Carolina Heritage 1808-2004*

For simplicity sake, please ignore any previously issued corrections for those listed below.

- On page 341, article # 952 on the second line states James Williamson died March 11, 1865. The correct date is April 11, 1865. This is according the American Civil War soldiers database on ancestry.com. It is also shown later in the article in the 5th paragraph.
- Page 46, article#142, paragraph 1, line 2: should be 10-29-1906.
- Page 51, article #175 for legend of a photo for Perth Amboy, should be for article #173.

Corrections submitted by Kathy McGuiness

Query

I am interested in receiving any available information from other descendants of my husband's ancestor, Duncan King (b. 1729, d. 1793) and his wife, Lydia Fosque (b. 1749, d. 1819). Please contact Ruth King at ruthk56@yahoo.com to share information, and place "Duncan King descendant" in the subject line.

Another Serving: Our Next Issue

Yes we have another heaping serving of Columbus County and Southeastern North Carolina miscellany in our next issue of *Columbus Chronicles*. Below is only a portion of the proposed menu. For inclusion in one of our issues, send your stories, tales, genealogies and history to the editor, Alice Soles, at CCLibrary@gmail.com.

Memories of My Bowen Grandparents
The Ralph and Bernice Harrelson Family
Balzura Wright Porter
Daddy's Garden of Love
Jonathan Lennon
Poems by Royce Ray

Spunky Loula
The Depression
Happy Father's Day
Hog Killing
Tobacco

--And Much, Much More!

IN MEMORIUM

Catherine Simmons Yates

Catherine Simmons came to the small town of Chadbourn, N.C. in 1948 to teach school shortly after she had graduated from W.C. U.N.C. in Greensboro, N.C. She became a popular high school teacher in the local high school. A few years after she came to live in Chadbourn, she met Dr. Robert Yates, a young hometown dentist. They were married in 1955 and she became Catherine Yates

Catherine S. Yates

Catherine had a great interest in the local history in and around Chadbourn, even though she came from another small North Carolina town, Massey Hill, located near Fayetteville. Her hometown area also had lots of historical lore, and Catherine kept her interest in this region too.

Catherine and Robert built a beautiful house on their property located just east of Chadbourn and began to raise their family. Their first son was aptly named Robert Allen Yates, Jr. A daughter, Lee, was born after Allen. By now of course Catherine had resigned from her teaching position and their time was given to the family, while Robert was the dentist in town, following some of his family's footsteps. Catherine's interest was her family, their church, Piney Forest Baptist and their many friends. She became involved in many civic organizations, and through these organizations she began her quest to learn as much as she could about her hometown, Chadbourn, and even the county, Columbus, where she now resided.

The late Miss Alice Lowe, an original member of the Sunny South Colony that had settled much earlier in Chadbourn, became great friends with Catherine. They worked closely together on various committees in local clubs, and Catherine's interest in local history became whetted even more after working with Miss Alice, who was known as the local historian in these parts.

Employed for many years with the original Waccamaw Bank and Trust Company, Miss Alice bequeathed all of the local written history, and all of the pictures that she had to Catherine Yates at her death. She knew that Catherine could, and would be the keeper of that precious history. Catherine, in turn did become the keeper of all of the valuable history she now possessed. Catherine did not stop with this collection, but continued to search and research the legacies and history in this area. She was always willing to share with anyone her articles, pictures and knowledge. If one needed to know something about our history it was only natural that one could just ask Catherine.

All the while, with Dr. Yates working with her, they became great supporters of our renowned Strawberry Festival which does bring some fame to our small town each year. In 1983, when our town celebrated its hundredth anniversary, Catherine researched and wrote a great pageant titled "A Town Growing With its People". The characters were from Chadbourn, and the play depicted the hundred years of Chadbourn's growth. Maybe some day we can have this play again. Catherine's shoes will be hard to fill in many aspects of this pageant.

Photograph curtsey of Gerri Lynn

CATHERINE SIMMONS YATES

CHADBOURN -- Catherine Simmons Yates, 78, died Friday, Nov. 9, 2007. She was the widow of Dr. Robert Allen Yates Sr., and the daughter of the late Tonnie Macob and Blanche Griggs Simmons.

A graveside service will be held at 2 p.m. Monday, Nov. 12, at Piney Forest Baptist Church Cemetery with the Rev. Hubert McCleney officiating. Worthington Funeral Home of Chadbourn is handling the arrangements.

Survivors include a son, Allen Yates and wife, Martha of Chadbourn; a daughter, Lee Yates McLean and her husband, Sammy of Angier; two brothers, T.M. "Sonny" Simmons of Fayetteville and Ernest G. Simmons of Fuquay-Varnina; a granddaughter, Jennifer Catherine McLean of Angier; and step-granddaughter, Courtney Clewis of Chadbourn.

Pallbearers will be John "Chuck" Simmons, Jimmy Simmons, Milton Blake, Keith Blake, John Blake, William Thompson, and Mack Ward.

Catherine and Robert donated their valuable collection of pictures they had of Chadbourn to the Library at the University of North Carolina in Chapel Hill, N. C. There they will be preserved and available to anyone who requests them.

Catherine loved flowers and I have never known anyone who had so many beautiful African Violets, and who could care for them, and who would share them with anyone for various occasions. Dr. Yates loved their yard, and their grapevines produced delectable grapes every year. He also had beehives that produced honey, and was a talented wood worker.

Catherine was a long time active member of the Southeastern North Carolina Genealogical Society. She served as the treasurer for many years in this organization and contributed much valuable information to the group. Catherine also had an avid interest in the Fair Bluff Historical Society and their Depot Museum. She also was active in the Lake Waccamaw Depot Museum

Dr Yates died in 2003 and Catherine died in December 2007. Surviving them are a son, Allen, his wife Martha; a daughter Lee and her husband, Sammy McLean ,a granddaughter, Jennifer Catherine McLean of Angier, and step-granddaughter, Courtney Clewis of Chadbourn. Two brothers survive Catherine, Sonny Simmons of Fayetteville and Ernest Simmons of Fuquay Varina.

Catherine was not a native daughter of Chadbourn or Columbus County, but through her sojourn that brought her this way, we all now have a greater knowledge and a greater appreciation for our heritage. This legacy has shaped all who knew her. She was truly a modern pioneer.

--Jimmie Sue Ward

Earl Williamson

A Biography of Lenworth Earl Williamson

--Jean Hood Williamson, March, 2008

L. Earl Williamson was an avid genealogist, an active member of the Southeastern North Carolina Genealogy Society, and staunch advocate for the production of this publication. Recently he passed away on June 29th, 2007, in Whiteville, North Carolina. He was buried on his 80th birthday.

L. Earl Williamson was born on July 1st, 1927 to his parents, Archie and Clara Elizabeth Martin Williamson, in Williamson's Crossroads, Chadbourn, (Columbus County), North Carolina. He was the eldest of five children, and the first in his family to have a formal education, it was indeed important to his being. His siblings were Charles Kenneth, Hilda Valenta Seary, Claire Elizabeth Stevens, and Neal Williamson.

The children did chores not unlike other children. Working in tobacco and picking strawberry's on their farm. Earl always spoke of picking strawberries as a great deal of fun, from the way he told this story, he ate as many as he picked. Their memories are lasting, and make for interesting stories in them selves. I believe their family is rather unique this day in time for they are all very close, in spirit and love.

He went to elementary school in Evergreen, North Carolina; high school in Portsmouth, Virginia; and college at Virginia Polytechnic Institute (VPI) in Blacksburg, Virginia. Earning a BS degree in Agronomy, he graduated in June, 1953. While attending high school in Portsmouth, Virginia, he often commented that he hated mathematics like so many young people do this day in time. He went on to say that one year he had the most wonderful teacher who made mathematics a game.

He moved to a front seat in that classroom, learning to have a great love for math the rest of his days, making up math games on his computer, and using it in his work with the USDA. His greatest wish in the last few years was that children in the classrooms of America could have a teacher like he did that made education fun.

Enlisting in the United States Navy July, 1944, he served on the training ship USS Wyoming and the USS Raven. He was discharged in June, 1946. While in college he spent his summers in the Merchant Marines as a cook and boatswain mate. A fun adventure for a young man!

L. E. WILLIAMSON, seamon second class, has returned to his post after spending a 10-day furlough with his parents, Mr. and Mrs. Archie Williamson, 107 Carolina avenue. Williamson volunteered last July and just recently completed his basic training at Camp Peary

Earl began working at his career for the USDA as a Soil Scientist in Richmond, Virginia, worked in Tappahannock, Virginia Beach and Southwest Virginia beginning in 1965. He retired in 1987 after 32 years of service to the Federal Government.

Loving his work, he did many things for the USDA: mapping the Blue Ridge Mountains when he was a young man in the service; survey work of Federal properties; cat fish ponds; worked with cattle, giving them shots; mapping out orchard groves and ditches for farmers, figuring the amount of soil to be removed. These are just a few positions that I can remember.

We celebrated 35 years together in a unique marriage. He and I both felt we were blessed to be able to have each other that long.

He was equally proud of my five children and his own two sons. They were the best part we had each brought to this union. My children are Deborah Jean (Baum) Jankiewicz, Steven Randolph Baum, Jacqueline Kay (Baum) Gearles, Lynn Hood Baum, and Deanna Leigh (Baum) King. All had grandsons for us to love and enjoy.

Earl taught these 11 grandsons, 2 step grandsons and 2 step granddaughters many things when they came to visit, or to baby-sit them as young children. He was immersed in their lives, once he wrote them all a letter at Christmas of how he believed they should live their lives as young adults.

They made little balsa wood cars together in his woodworking shop after he retired, but most of all they absolutely loved "their Grandpa" to teach them things about the water: sailing, boating, tying knots, skiing, etc. Earl was endeared to each of these children, taking them under his wings as a Step Grandpa.

He had two brilliant children from his first marriage, Michael Stephen and Paul Gregory. Michael had a career in acting with performances on Broadway in New York City and summer stock. His thesis of Shakespeare's play was written, choreographed and acted by Michael for his Masters Degree at Ohio State University. Unfortunately, he passed away in 1995 at the age of 42. Paul graduated from William & Mary University in Virginia, joined the United States Army, studied linguistics in California, and became an interpreter of German and Russian languages while stationed in Germany. Presently he is a computer writer, working on his Master's degree. They had/have terrific careers; their father was proud of his sons and their accomplishments.

Paul and his wife recently had children, two little girls, Prithia and Charlotte. Earl finally had granddaughters of his own. Unfortunately he passed away before he met the last child. She will grow up knowing of her grandfather, and the many stories he had to tell.

We have been fortunate enough to have a dear little couple with a young daughter next door to us. Hannah's grandparents live away from Columbus County. Therefore, she adopted Earl as her "Grand Papa". Together they had a special relationship. She loved for him to play in the lake with her, observing her while she was learning to swim. That thrilled him! His life was all about learning and teaching others what he knew.

Earl was a former member of Macedonia Baptist Church, Williamsons Crossroads, and a member of Lake Waccamaw Presbyterian Church in Lake Waccamaw, North Carolina.

We moved to Lake Waccamaw in 1995. Before then, we came to the lake to vacation, sail, swim, and enjoy the wonderful farm veggies and fruits. The family jokes about the way he went shopping at the Farmers Market, he always came home with bushels of corn, greens, tomatoes etc. for me to cook or preserve for the coming year. Each time he went there, I would plead with him just to bring enough for a few days. It had to be the "Ag thing" with Earl, for he just laughed with, and at me, upon coming in the kitchen. Later years he did try to help quite a bit, with the freezing and canning, loving every moment.

Earl served as Vice President of our local Southeastern North Carolina Genealogy Society, and also on the committee for the Columbus County Heritage Book. The genealogy and stories held dear by the words of the people comprised in this book, Earl had lived beside, gone away from, and came back home too. He was all about genealogy, leaving behind, large bins of genealogy; he had worked on since the early 1980's. He ate, slept and talked about this "material" constantly; loving; knowing about his families, their past/present lives, as well as the history of ancestors.

He was taken ill with lung cancer in 1995, had three major lung surgeries, plus melanoma two years before he passed away. Talk about a positive person, he lived for 13 years with these illnesses; yet he still took a swim during the summer months every day in the lake if he was able, traveled to California to see the children as well as Virginia and Maryland. What a survivor! Later, after he passed away, we found these items written by him; a Diary named "*Earl's Book*", and a book named, "*You Can Do It*", a book of positive thinking.

It is wonderful for all our family to have these treasured memories; definitely a colorful fellow, loving each day he lived. When we moved back permanently to the lake from a large city, Earl was just getting over the second lung surgery. He sat in the swing on the front porch overlooking Lake Waccamaw saying to me, "I cannot imagine not living at the lake".

I sincerely believe this lake, and the people of this community helped in God's plan to heal him. As he sat in his rocking chair/swing on the porch, folks would wander by stopping to visit with him (not always entering the porch, just chatting while standing in the yard) he discussed many things in his "front porch" conversations such as recipes, sailing, church, news of people in the community, etc. In his last days, I rolled him out to the front porch in a wheel chair in order for him to see the lake and the people in the community. It made him very happy! Our front porch was a blessing, a healing in some ways to both of us, as well as our neighbors.

Several months ago, one of our children said they wanted to jot down all the suggestions Earl made constantly to everyone making it into a book, believing it might be a good seller. He continually told everyone in the family his suggestions of how they should do things. My, what a book that would have been! Our family nicknamed him "Earl the Pearl". He was a "Pearl" of a fellow!

Mama's Cow – The Golden Guernsey

Oral History by Earl Williamson
Written by Kathleen McGuiness, June 18, 2007

The journey started with a Guernsey cow in the midst of the Great Depression in 1938. Columbus County North Carolina was and is mainly a farming area. Archie and Clara Martin Williamson, with their then four children, were farmers. They lived on a farm called the Mays' Place. The times were very hard for them. They had no horse or vehicle for travel other than a mule and wagon. Both had lost their mothers as children and their fathers had remarried. The result was that they had no inherited land to live on. Archie had met Clara Martin while she was enrolled in Nurses Training School in Marion County S.C. They fell in love and had married on August 5, 1926.

The Macedonia Baptist Church was central to them, their relatives and neighbors. Everyone looked out for the other. Archie had an uncle, Richard Holmes Edmund, who traded in livestock. Archie bought a Guernsey cow from him for a low price. This cow provided two gallons of milk twice a day. Clara milked this cow and churned their butter. The family had plenty of milk, butter, buttermilk and cornbread. There was the occasional wild hog for butchering. The men who went out hunting together shared the fresh meat. The family had plenty of vegetables from their garden for their own table and sharing with others. Daughters Hilda and Claire Elizabeth spent many happy hours with their mother canning these veggies and preserving jams from grapes.

Mama's Cow – The Golden Guernsey

Clara had her eye on a fifteen acre farm which was owned by Cornie Wynn Williamson, a cousin of Archie's. Today Reverend Vernon Williamson lives on this property located on Princess Anne Road. One Sunday morning after church Clara walked a mile and a half to Cornie Wynn's home. She bravely made a proposition for her family. They would buy the fifteen acre farm with only the cow, worth seventy five dollars, as down payment. The offer was accepted and Cornie Wynn provided the mortgage. On September 22, 1938 they became land owners.

A home still had to be made, however. Standing on this farm was a tobacco pack house about 16 ft. by 20 ft., a mule barn and a corn shed. Archie bought some lumber and built a kitchen onto the side of the pack house. The walls of the pack house were just boards nailed together, no insulation. So they pasted up cardboard and newspaper sheets on the walls. They used the tobacco's burlap sheets as a room divider. There was a cast iron wood burning stove for the kitchen. A homemade wood burning 50 gallon metal heater with a flute stood next to the wall in the other room. Since the heater was tin it would turn red hot when used. Clara made their mattresses with the dried shucks from the corn. They finally had their own home.

The people back then had stove wood cutting parties. You would go to a neighbor's home with your crosscut saw. The men would cut down a few pine trees, cutting them into stove wood lengths. Later this wood would be split up by the owner. Refreshments from a jug were available for the workers. This would be followed by a large meal prepared by the women.

Archie and Clara's last child, Neal, was born in this "pack" house in 1939 with the help of a midwife. The doctor arrived later in the day.

In the fall of 1939 the family moved to Portsmouth, Virginia. Archie found a job working as a carpenter for five dollars a day at the chemical plant there. The families of Archie's sisters Jesse Britt, Vera Freedman and Blanche Brown had already moved there, as their husbands also had jobs there. Mr. Charles Harper owned a large number of houses in Pinners Point Va. He hired Archie to work on the side, painting and hanging wallpaper. He then sold them a house on Pinners Avenue with no down payment. They rehabbed the house, made improvements, and hung wallpaper. The family was able to sell it for a profit. They did this flipping of homes five times. Now they were able to buy a house for cash on Hamilton Avenue in Portsmouth.

During this time Archie was hired by the railroad. They still had family ties to Columbus County, N.C., however. In 1946 his cousin Ludie Williamson wrote to Archie about the sale of the Kallihan farm. Archie called the owner on the phone and asked him to hold it for him. Archie made a quick sale on his house in Va. and came to Columbus County with the money. His oldest sons Earl and Kenneth "C.K." contributed money towards it which made it possible for Archie and Clara to buy this farm. Their special cousin Sam Williamson and family farmed Archie's "Kallihan" land while they continued to live in Portsmouth.

In the summers, Clara with her children, Claire Elizabeth and Neal, traveled to the farm on their railroad passes. They graded and tied their share of the tobacco crop that Sam had farmed. The tobacco had to be picked from the bottom of the plant and tied in groups to be hung for a five day drying process. Then the leaves were separated by their grade and stacked in piles. They all worked hard but they also enjoyed themselves. There were swims in the river, visits with a multitude of cousins "down the road", as well as fishing and cookouts all summer long by the Lumber River.

In the post World War II period the railroad business was slacking off. Archie was laid off from 1949 to 1953. The family then returned to their N.C. farm, their ace in the hole, resuming the farming life. Archie had help from Clara's brother Coy Martin, cousin Troy Williamson and their son C.K. to build a small house there. He then was rehired by the railroad and they moved back to Portsmouth. During the 1950's there were several moves back and forth. By this time the four older children Earl, Kenneth, Hilda and Claire Elizabeth were married and living in Virginia. When their son Neal got married in 1959 they sold their Virginia house to him.

In 1962 Archie had another lay off for about two years and moved back to N.C. They then decided to sell their "Kallihan" farm for $10,000 and bought a 90 acre farm in Bladenboro for $20,000. This farm came with a tractor and other farm equipment. The soil was better for farming than their previous land. It was just a few miles outside of town. There was an old green house that had been a tenant house. It did not have a kitchen or bathroom inside.

Later, Archie and Clara made their final move back to Portsmouth Va. In 1970 after 30 years with the railroad he retired as an engineer. Archie had enjoyed driving both the steam and diesel engine trains. Now it was time for retirement and to live where they were happiest.

In 1971 Archie and Clara moved back to their hometown in Tatum Township, Columbus County. They lived on the "Pearlie Place", named for previous owner Pearl Martin Williamson, widow of John Devon Williamson. This farm on Princess Ann Road had been bought by their son Neal in 1968. The property had an old house on it. This land title goes all the way back to Archie and John Devon Williamson's ancestor, Joshua Williamson, who was born in 1775.

Archie and Clara still owned their Bladenboro farm, however. It was being farmed by others. They sold this farm to their children Earl, Hilda and Claire Elizabeth. With the proceeds from that transaction they purchased a three acre property from the widow Ethel Martin in 1974. Ethel had been the wife of James Stephen Martin, Clara's first cousin. The family built a new brick house there.

Archie and Clara enjoyed furnishing their retirement home with new furniture. Here they had a large 50th Wedding Anniversary celebration with many family members and friends. They loved visits with their many grandchildren from Virginia and Florida. This was where they spent their final days, back home in Tatum Township, Columbus County, North Carolina. Their good fortunes can be traced back to the efforts of the young Clara the gutsy country business woman, who traded the Guernsey cow for their first piece of land.

Memories of Earl Williamson

My father was always full of curiosity, had a desire to learn; about the changing world, technology, and about people. He was very interested in others and was always willing to listen to what they had to say. Perhaps, for this reason, he could get along so well with anyone, even if he had just met them.

He treated everyone as if they were an old friend. He was fun to be around, and had a joyful sense of humor. He, like everyone else, suffered from his flaws and disappointments; but the essence of his life was that he loved it, and loved being with the people in his life."
-- Paul Gregory Williamson

My Big Brother Earl, My Hero

Growing up with Earl was wonderful. He was handsome, fun, and I could always count on him.

Earl liked the outdoors; fishing, camping, swimming, biking and, boating. He loved woodworking; he made beautiful furniture and all kinds of different pieces. He loved learning anything new and attended school his entire life. Just before he passed away he was learning Spanish. He taught his sons, sisters, nieces, nephews, step children, grandchildren, friends and others families to sail and water ski.

We were a very close family, he is sorely missed.   -- Hilda Williamson Seary

What I Remember About My Step-Father, Earl

What I remembered the most about Earl was that he enjoyed eating, and talking about food. How it was made and, what the ingredients were. He especially liked anything with lemon in it.
-- Jacqueline Baum Gearles

Fondest Memories of My Step-Father, Earl

In my younger days, Earl was tough on me, as he really wanted to make sure that I could take care of myself as an adult. I grew up, married, and had children. He truly loved the babies; he could hold them for hours, feed them, and even changed a diaper or two. He did not mind. I believe loving the grandkids kept him young. The kids loved him right back as well.

My fondest memories as an adult are going to garage sales with Earl, as he like me, was always wanting to score at a garage sale (getting the best of the best deals). Earl would sleep in everyday, but not when he was at our home, and it was a garage sale day. I would get up early, he would already be sitting at the kitchen counter waiting to go, wouldn't even eat, as we would eat on the road, getting a cup of coffee and go. Earl loved getting books at the garage sales, he couldn't get enough of them.

–Deanna Baum King

Cousins

Earl and I were cousins, not as close on the Williamson side as we were on the Martin side. His Martin grandfather, Cornelius, and my Martin great-grandfather, S. Mitchell, were brothers. Earl and I would see each other occasionally while he lived in Virginia, but after he retired and moved to Lake Waccamaw, we each joined the Southeastern North Carolina Genealogical Society. Then we really shared lots of family history and stories. Earl worked diligently on his family genealogy and, was thrilled to share it with others. Yes, he even shared a few recipes with me of things he found tasty. This past summer Earl was put to rest in a place that he dearly loved and, enjoyed visiting, Macedonia Baptist Church Cemetery.

-- Betty Branch

Earl's Curiosity

We admired Earl's intellectual curiosity. He was interested in learning about a lot of different things, and he wanted to know the truth, not just the hype. Although he lived most of his adult life away from Columbus County, he enjoyed coming back to his roots. And he deeply valued two of the most precious natural resources of Columbus County--the Lumber River and Lake Waccamaw.

We enjoyed canoeing with Earl and his grandsons on the Lumber and sailing with him on Lake Waccamaw. In our opinion, he truly valued what is best in Columbus County—its beautiful natural waterways and its down-to-earth honest, hardworking people. We loved being able to call Earl our friend.

-- David and Donna Scott

Grandpa Earl

Grandpa and I loved to make cookies together, even the one's that did not turn out right. Grandpa and I still ate them.

I loved going out on the lake with Grandpa in the boats, but my favorite was the pontoon boat, because he let me drive it all by myself.

-- Taylor King

Grandpa Earl

The first thing that pops into my head about my Grandpa Earl is his toothy grin, especially when he knew someone was taking his picture, or when he thought something was truly funny. The fondest memories of Grandpa Earl almost always include a body of water, that's one love we both shared. I still have pictures/images in my head of my first sailing adventure with him. When I looked at him as a young boy he had black sunglasses that reflected the water, a sailor hat on his head. With the wind whipping he lost the hat to the lake. He showed me how to turn the sailboat around, then we went and scooped it out of the water.

I believe his proudest moments with all of the grandchildren was teaching us to love the things he loved, especially how to become successful, and hopefully become a doctor or stock broker someday! But, the most coveted memory of my grandfather was when I was old enough to truly understand how his mind worked, and the things he really felt. He mostly discussed these things when it was just the two of us. I recall going to visit my grandmamma and him one summer. A storm was coming; they needed some extra help around the house. After that night, he and I went for a swim at night in the lake, it was warm outside, very peaceful. We talked about families, responsibility and such, knowing that when he was coming of age it has been a much harder life. It made me appreciate what he went through, and how easy we sometimes have it in our lives. It was a memory I will hold forever.

--Timothy Randolph Gearles

Memories of Earl

Earl had a love for food, so much so, that he would try all food, and find out where it came from. He may not have liked something that he tasted, but he would try it to learn more.

I liked his inquisitiveness to ask questions, and to get your true thoughts of what was important to you and why. -- Doug A. King

Memories of Earl Williamson

Although Earl and I shared a surname, and a Y chromosome from a common ancestor (Lewis Williamson, before 1750 – about 1799), and even grew up within 25 miles of each other. we did not meet until November 2000.

Once we got to know each other, we shared some great times discussing Williamson family history. When I first arranged to visit Earl at this home in Lake Waccamaw, he suggested that, on the way down, I swing by Macedonia Baptist Church to walk through the cemetery and "visit some of my ancestors". Was I ever amazed? There are so many Williamsons buried there! I had four rolls of film – 24 frames per roll – but had to go into Cerro Gordo to get more. Earl knew I would arrive at his house later than I had expected, so he went for a boat ride on the lake, his favorite activity.

-- Dr. John H. Williamson, Davidson, North Carolina

Index

See also Former Employees of Acme Fertilizer Manufacturing Company on page 8. **Bold** indicates a subject of a major article. *Italics* indicate an illustration.

Acme, 6
Acme Fertilizer Manufacturing Company, 6-9
Alford: Mary Eliza, 37; Priscilla, 38
Allen: Anna C., 47; Charles A., 47; Cora M., 47; Elizabeth. *See* Wooton, Elizabeth Allen; Elva M.. *See* Newland, Elva M. Allen; George E., 47; Helen B., 47; Henry, 47; Ida, 47; James A., 47; Wilbur A., 47
Alliance Hall, 30
Amboy: Perth, 51
Andrews: Bertha. *See* Grassie, Bertha Pifer Andrews
Arnette: James Robert, 14; Laura Jane Rowell, 14; Nancy Elizabeth. *See* Miller, Nancy Elizabeth Arnette
Arp: Dorothy Lee. *See* Miller, Dorothy Lee Arp; Eliza (Ressie) Watts, 13; William Rhader, 13
Atlantic Coast Line Railroad, 5
Avant & Sholar, 25
Baggett: Mrs., 25
Bailey: Clare Russell, 47; Cornelia Robinson, 40, 48; Dorothy Elliot, 47; Earl Russell, 48; Elizabeth E. Smith, 47; Elroy Byron, 40, 47, 48; Guy Loey, 47; Leon A., 40, 48; Loey Robinson, 40; Lowy Robinson, 48; Myrtle A. Clark, 47; Myrtle M. Jolly, 47; Oprah Koonce, 47; Rena Duncan, 40; Rene Duncan, 48; Russell Z., **40**, 47, 48; Wayne Elroy, 47
Baird: Annie. *See* Boughner, Annie
Baldwin: Margaret. *See* Moyers, Margaret Baldwin; Morgan, 18; Olivia. *See* Wilson, Olivia Baldwin; Ruth, 18; Sarah. *See* Inman, Sarah Baldwin Bryan
Ballard: W. S., Rev., 28
Barber: John E., 48
Barefoot: ?, *28*
Bartley: Dan, *32*

Batten: Millie T., *16*
Battle of Moore's Creek Bridge, 10
Battle of New Bern, 11
Baysden: David, 25
Beaver Dam, 5
Benton: Ashley, 31, 32
Best: Fanny Warren Smith, 20; Gaston, 20
Betsyburg, 20
Black: Naomi. *See* White, Naomi Black; Sam, 17
Black Creek Primitive Baptist Church, 44
Black Creek School, 44
Black Rock, 5
Blake: Dora, 29
Blanchard: Latha, *28*
Blanton: Ellen Watts, 39
Bogue Chapel Baptist Church, 16
Bogue Swamp, 16, 30
Bolin: Clara Blue. *See* Miller, Clara Blue Bolin
Boswell: Eli, 37; English Devon, 39; Lizzie Wright, 39; Susannah (Susie) Long, **37**
Boughner: Annie, 48; Fannie. *See* Crawford, Fannie Boughner ; George Hemperley, 48; Grace Elizabeth. *See* Elvington, Grace Elizabeth Boughner ; Leota. *See* Cain, Leota Boughner ; Nellie J. Boughner. *See* Miller, Nellie J. Boughner ; Ruth. *See* Nye, Ruth Boughner
Brady: Alfred B., Sr., 49; Maude Eula Moors, 49
Branch: Betty W., 45; Charles, *32*
Braunstein: Richard, Rev., 12
Britt: Billy, *32*
Broderick: W. E., 30
Brooks: Billy, *32*
Brown: Alice H.. *See* Newland, Alice H. Brown; Baldwin, 15, 16, **22**, 25; Bessie, 28, *29*; Betty Lennon, 15; James A., 49; Joseph A., 47; Margaret. *See* Wilson, Margaret Brown; Mary Lou, *16*, 28, *29*; Patience. *See* Newland, Patience Brown;

R. E. Lee, 47; Sallie "Aunt Sally", 17, *17*, **24 - 27**, *26*, 28, *29*; Valery, 28
Bruton: Beth Spivey McMillan, **38**; Bill, 38
Bryan: Jonathan, 34; William, **34**
Bullard: Alexander, 14; Alexander Wesley, 14; Hattie Ophelia Bullard. *See* Preston, Hattie Ophelia Bullard; Helen Hammond, 14; Mary Hattie Miller, 14
Byrd: James, Mrs. (Pifer), 50
C. M. Cox Store, 41
Cain: Leota Boughner, 48; Samuel Ernest, 48
Caldwell: Ola, 30
Camp: William, 34
Campbell: Rev., 28
Cape Fear, 5
Carolina Central Railroad, 5
Carroll: Grace, 18
Casey: Laura, 48; Morton, 48; Morton Peterson, 48; Randel, 48; Thomas, 48; Viola, 48
Caswell: Richard, Col., 10
Chadbourn, *47*, 52
Chadbourn Baptist Church, 47
Chapin: Emily A., 48; John, 48
Charleston Earthquake, 43, 44
Chauncey: Annie Belle, 17; Clarence, 17; Mary Lou, 17; Nick, 17
Chillson: Elizabeth Allen. *See* Payne, Elizabeth Allen Chillson
Clark: Myrtle A.. *See* Bailey, Myrtle A. Clark; Sallie. *See* Wooten, Sallie Clark
Clemmons: Elbert, 18
Clewis: Courtney, 53
Cobb: T. J., Rev., 28
Colburn: Chas L., 48; Harriette, 48
Collier: Clyde, 24
Columbus Theatre, 3
Corvil: Lottie Whitney, 50
Coultas: Alvin, 51; Alvin Foster, 48; Catherine Lena, 48; Elizabeth, 48; Elizabeth

Rebecca, *See* Miller, Elizabeth Rebecca; Frank E., 48; Gertrude Rush, 48; Marian Francis, *See* Robertson, Marian Francis; Nora, 48; Pauline Lois, 48
Council: Arthur, *10*; Jessie Wooten, *10*
Council's Ridge, 20
Covil: William Edward, 50
Cox: Charlie Marshall, **41**; Isaac, 38; Martha Louvina, 38; Molcey Stanley, 38; Tempie Jane Norris, **41**
Crawford: C. B., 48; Fannie Boughner, 48; Jim, *17*; Kate, 20
Cronly: Michael, 5
Cronly Manufacturing Company, 6
Currie: Mary. *See* Sears, Mary Currie; Nellie, 13
Davis: Elvira. *See* Wooten, Elvira Davis; Jennie, 25; Sarah Elvira. *See* Wooten, Sarah Elvira; Willie, *10*
Delco, 9
Dixon: Jim, 31
Dow: David, 31
Duncan: Rena. *See* Bailey, Rena Duncan
Dupree Landing, 17. 28
Edwards: Carl, 37; Tommy, *32*
Elbow, 30
Elliot: Dorothy. *See* Bailey, Dorothy Elliot
Elvington: Grace Elizabeth, 48
Evergreen, **31**
Evergreen Baptist Church, 31
Fair Bluff Depot Museum, 53
Fair Bluff Historical Society, 53
Farmer's Day, **3**
Farmers Alliance Hall, 30
Faulk: Martha Lucinda. *See* Norris, Martha Lucinda Faulk
Fea: daughter, 48, *See* Gallagher, Mrs. James; Edna L., 48, *See* Stephens, Edna L.; George, 48; Lydia, 48
Fields: Frederick, 33; Simpson C., 31; Vance, 32, **33**
Fipps: Dow, 37
First Methodist Church of Evergreen, 31

Floy: Lou. *See* Milligan, Lou Floy Watts
Formyduval: Linnie, 15
Formy-Duval: Theresa, 19
Foster: Chas W., 48; Nellie, 48
Fowler: Alfred S., **39**; Anna Wright, 38; Edith, 39; James "Jim", 39; Lydia, 39; Mary Ann Watts, 39
Fowler Town, 38, 39
Freedman: George or Joseph, 48; George Washington, 48; Johanna, 48; John D., 48; Joseph, 48; Mary (Mattie), 48; Stephen, 48; Wilmer Brice, 48
Freeman: Benjamin, 34
Frink: Ethel, *28*
Games, 45
Gause: Elizabeth Rose, 12; Rose. *See* Memory, Rose Gause
Gerald: Annie Jean, 37
Gilbert: Sheriff, 26
Gilchrist: William, 6
Glendale Baptist Church, 35
Glenn: David, *16*
Godwin: Charlie, 24; Jess, 24; Mabel, 24
Gonser: Albert, 48
Gonzer: Charlotte, 48
Goode: Mabel, 30
Goodrich: 15. Herman R., 48; Chas B., 48; Florence L. Moors, 48; Francie B., 48
Grange Farm, 5
Grassie: Bertha Pifer Andrews, 50
Griffin: Columbus, 31; Frank, 31
Griffin Crossroads, 31
Griffin's Crossroads Baptist Church, 31
Grissett Swamp, 44
Grissette: Charity Wooten, 10, 11; George Reuben, 11
Hall: John William, 12
Hallsboro, 14, 26, 30
Hallsboro Baptist Church, 12, 17, 28
Hallsboro High School, 18
Hallsboro Methodist Church, 12, 28
Hamandz: Jessie S., 49; May, 49
Hammond: Charlotte Lottie. *See* Miller, Charlotte Lottie Hammond; Harriet Thompson, 12; Helen. *See* Bullard, Helen Hammond; Nathan, 12

Hampton: Benjamin, 48; Benjamin Moran (Reginia), 48; Mary Ann Morgan, 48; Wade, 17
Hand: Amber Louise Moors, 49; Evans Sanford, 49
Hardee: Crance, **35**; Kathleen Mishoe, 35
Harnly: Benjamin E., 49; Harold Shepard, 49
Harnly or Harnley: Benjamin Hoerner, 49
Hawfield's Cemetery, **47**
Hayes: Callie, 26
Hedgepath: Betty Walker, 40
Hedgepeth: Roland, Rev., 28
Hewitt: Gertrude. *See* Newland, Gertrude Hewitt
Hicks: C. B. Rev., 13
High: Darcus, 27; Hubert "Shine", 27; Mary, 25
Hinson: Ann, 39
Hodge: Mime, 38
Holcomb: Charles, 13; Eleanora Pinner, 12; Frank, 13; James Wesley, 12; Nancy, 14; Nancy Bogan. *See* Miller, Nancy Bogan Holcomb; Vander, 13
Holland: Jean Elizabeth Strole, 51; Richardson, Edward Jr., 51
Holmes: Dew, *16*
Horton: G. E., 49; Martha, 49
Howe: Bertha. *See* Usher, Bertha Howe; Jedediah V., 51; Jedediah V. (J. V.), 49; Zillah, 49
Illion, 31
Illion Supply Company, 31
Inman: Hardy, 34; Sarah Baldwin Byran, 34; Ted, *32*
Iron Hill Store, 37
Ivey: Creasy Ivey. *See* Stone, Creasy Ivey
Jackson: Pecola, 15
Jacobs: Dunk, 24; Ida, 24; Kitsey Bell, 38
Johnson: Bill, *32*; Jerry, *32*; Leggett, *32*; Thomas Ray, *32*; William O. "Bill", *32*
Jolly: Myrtle M.. *See* Bailey, Myrtle M. Jolly
Jones: Rita Diane Stevens, **41**
Joyner: Sis, 38
Keaton: Earnestine, 5
Kelly: H. N., 29

Kerchne: F. W., 47
Keyser: Ronald, Rev., 12
King: Nancy Holcomb White, 13; Thelton Gleen, 13
Koonce: Oprah. See Bailey, Oprah
Lake Waccamaw, 17, *26*
Lake Waccamaw Depot Museum, 53
Lattimore: William, 6
Leders Department Store, 20
Lennon: Ann R., 31; Betty. See Brown, Betty Lennon; Dennis S., Jr., 31; Dennis Stephen, 31; Denver, *32*; G. P., 31; Hanna H.. See Nance, Hannah H. Lennon; Hartford D., 31; J. I., 31; J. P., 31; John Cale, 31; Lott B., 31; Orrie, 31; Rosser Yates, 31; Sallie J., 31
Lennon, Dennis, 32
Leonhart: Agnes. See Moors, Agnes Leonhart; Agnes Rattray, 49; Charles Rattray, 49; Ida Louise, 49; Martin Francis, 49
Lewis: Tommy, *32*
Linn: Harriette (Hattie). See Howe, Harriette (Hattie) Linn
Little Iron Hill Run, 37
Little Sugarloaf Plantation, 11
Livingston, 5
Livingston Creek, 5
Lloyd Landing, 5
Loman: Ada Lillian, 49; George Franklin, 49; Rachel Maria, 49; Samuel, 49; Samuel T., 49; Superia Agnes, 49
Long: Eva Lillian Miller, 14; Joshua, **37**; Mary Eliza Alford, 37; William Melvin, 14
Loris Clinic, 35
Lowe: Alice, 52
Lufkin: Daniel M., 49; Elizabeth, 49
Lynn: Kenneth George Swift, 13; Penny Kay White, 13; Ruby Mae, 13
Maggie Mae an infant, 37
Manning: Emily. See Walker, Emily Manning
Marlowe: J. M., Rev., 28
Martin: Clara Elizabeth. See Williamson, Clara Elizabeth

Martin; Cornelius, 57; S. Mitchell, 57
Massey Hill, 52
Matthews: Arnette, 51; Rachel Estelle Strole, 51
Maultsby: Helen, *17*
McCallum: Ida. See Wooten, Ida McCallum
McDougald: Juanita, 19
McIntrye: J. B. (Judge), 20
McKenzie: Mrs., 25
McLean: Lee Yates, 52; Sammy, 53
McMillan: Beth Spivey, 38; John, 38
McQueen: Clarie Amma White, 13; Robert Merlin, 13
McWhorter: Frank Edward, 13; Marion H. White, 13
Memory: Rose Gause, *10*
Mercer: Doc, 47
Merritt: Margaret, 18; Wilbur, 19
Middleton: Margaret (Maggie) Lou. See Newland, Margaret (Maggie) Lou Middleton
Mill Branch Primitive Baptist Church, **43**, 44
Miller: Alice Scott, 14; Benjamin Abner, 14; Benjamin Abner "Ab", 12; Bruce, 14; Charles Benjamin, 12; Charles Marselle, 13; Charlotte Lottie Hammond, 12; Clara Blue Bolin, 14; Clyde Pittman, 14; Coon, 14; David, 14; Dorothy Lee Arp, 13; Earl W., Sr, 48; Elbert Monroe, 14; Elizabeth Rebecca, 48; Ellen Stone, 12; Guilford Preston, 12; James Blaylock, 14; James R., 48; Jesse, 12; John Clarendon, 12; Joseph, 14; Lacy, 14; Lawrence, 14; Leroy, 14; Marvin, 14; Mary, 12; Mary Hattie Miller. See Bullard, Mary Hattie Miller; Mary Sadler. See White, Mary Sadler Miller; Nancy Arnette. See Carlisle, Nancy Arnette Miller; Nancy Bogan Holcomb, 12; Nancy Elizabeth Arnette, 14; Nellie J. Boughner, 48; Paul, 14; Phillip, 14; Pittman, **12**; Ralph, 14; Raymond McNeil, 14; Robert Lee, 14; Ruby Ethel

Tyler, 14; Terry Teddy, 13; Woodrow Wilson, 14
Milligan: Lou Floy Watts, 35
Minos Meares Road, 43
Mishoe: Kathleen, 35
Missionary Baptist Church, Evergreen, 31
Mitchell: John, 26
Mollie, 39
Moore: Nathaniel, 5
Moors: Agnes Leonhart, 49; Amanda A., 49; Amber Louise. See Hand, Amber Louise Moors; Bryon, 49; Florence L.. See Florence L. Moors Goodrich; Maude Eula. See Brady, Maude Eula Moors; Rufus King, 49
Morgan: Mary Ann. See Hampton, Mary Ann Morgan
Morphis: Elizabeth. See Wooten, Elizabeth Morphis
Morris: Wilkes, 5
Moskow: Mrs., 20
Moskow's Department Store, 20
Moyers: Margaret Baldwin, 18
Mt. Tabor, 44
Nance: Enoch, 31; Hannah H. Lennon, 31; Will, *32*
Navassa Guano Company, 5
New Life Church Community, 35
Newland: Charles Benjamin, 49; Elva M. Allen, 47; Estelle May. See Pittman, Estelle May Newland; Fannie Rosalia, 49; Gertrude Hewitt, 49; Harry Taylor, 49; James Tate, 49; Leroy Tate, Dr., 49; Patience Brown, 49; Robert M., 47; Robert Melvin, 49; Willard, 49
Norris: Martha Lucinda Faulk, 41; Patricia Wilson, 15; Priscilla Alford, 38; Prudence, 38; Sarah, 38; Tempie Jane. See Cox, Tempie Jane Norris; William, Jr., 38
Nye: Rubie, 48; William Baird, 48
Oliver: Sarah Lucy. See Wooten, Sarah Lucy Oliver
Panish: Emma, 49
Parker: Carrie, Rev., 13; Eliza, 18, 29
Parkin: J. C., 32
Parkton, 46

Patrick: Charlie, 9
Payne: Dodge S., 50; Dodge Sweet, 50; Elizabeth Allen Chillson, 50; Fred H., 50; Glenn W., 50; Hope, 50; Lizzie R., 50; Sarah M., 50
Peacock Road, 43
Pearsall: Nancy White King, 14; S. Carroll, 47; Stephen Carroll, 12
Perrin: Fannie (Annie), 50; Josiah (Joseph), 50
Pierce: Alma, 18; Clarkie, 18; Edelle, 18; Frances, *16*, **46**; John Edward, 17; Kate, *17*; Lillian, 18; Lonnie, 18; Nora, *17*; Ola, 16; Randolph, *17*; Sophia, *16*; Tecumseh, 17
Pierce and Company, 26
Pierce Cemetery, **46**
Pierce School, Hallsboro, N.C., *29*
Pifer: Clara. *See* Smith, Clara Pifer; Elwood A., 50; Mary E. Zigler, 50; Roy, 50; Somerton, 50; Willis, 50
Piney Forest Baptist Church, 52
Piney Woods, 5
Pinner: Eleanora. *See* Holcomb, Eleanora Pinner
Pireway Primitive Baptist Church, 44
Pittman: Estelle May Newland, 50
Porter: Angelo, Rev., 28; Balzura Wright, 37, 38; James Albert, 37; Samuel J., Dr., 28
Powell: Carson, 31; Harvey, **35**; Mary Watts, 35; Vester, 35; William L., *16*
Preston: Hattie Ophelia Bullard, 12
Primitive Baptist Church, 37
Ramsbottom: Bernice, 50; Gladys, 50; Lena, 50; Thomas H., 51; Thomas Hadden, 50
Rattray: Agnes. *See* Leonhart, Agnes Rattray
Ray: Lloyd, *28*
Ray, Bennett, 30
Redbug, **30**
Red Bug School, 18
Redbug School District 5, 30
Reid: Celestia, 50; G. S., 50
Reynolds: B. S., 6

Richardson: Mrs., 18
Riegelwood, NC, 5
Rivenbark: Alice, **40**; Crowell, 40; Theodore, **40**
Robertson: John Paul, 48
Robeson: J. P., 5
Robertson, Marian Francis, 48
Robinson: Cornelia. *See* Bailey, Cornelia Robinson, *See* Bailey, Corrnelia Robinson, Rogers: Dixie Wilson, 27; Dixie Wilson 15 - 24; Dr., 35; George, 46
Rogers,: Kit, **36**
Rowell: Laura Jane. *See* Arnette, Laura Jane Rowell
Rows: Charlie, 17
Sadler: R. C., Dr., 13
Scott: Alice. *See* Miller, Alice Scott
Sears: Mary Currie, 46
Shaver: John, 50, 51; John H., 50; Joseph S., 50; Robert, 50; Santa or Sinda L., 50; SantaAda, 50; T. A., 50
Shaw: Irene Brown, *28,* **28 - 34**; Margaret Brown, *17*
Short and Beers Lumber Mill, *33*
Simmons: Catherine. *See* Yates, Catherine Simmons; Ernest, 53; Sonny, 53
Simpson Creek Primitive Baptist Church, 44
Singletary: Mary (Duhadway). *See* Wooten, Mary (Duhadway) Singletary
Skipper: Lloyd, **40**; Slade, 40
Smith: Alvie, 13; Arthur, Mrs.. *See* Smith, Clara Pifer; Clara Pifer, 50; Elizabeth, 19; Elizabeth E. *See* Bailey, Elizabeth E. Smith; Fanny Warren. *See* Best, Fanny Warren Smith; Ferry Gertrude. *See* White, Ferry Gertrude Smith; G. Herbert, 6; George Calvin, 39; Jerome, Rev. Dr., 39; Lillie, 18; Maggie, *16*
Smithman: David, 50; Elsie L., 50; Ernest D., 50; Herbert, 50; Lucy G., 50; Mable A., 50; Mary H., 50; Sepan L., 50
Soles: Alice, 1, 2; Anna Eliza Watts, 38; Armegy R., **38**; Calvin, **37**; Charles, 37; Duff, 37; James Barliver "Bud", 38;

Jordan "Jird", 38; Martha Louvina Cox, 38; R. C. Jr., 37; R. C. Sr., 37; Sarah "Sis", 38; Wallace, 37
Soles and Company, C. C., 37
Southeastern North Carolina Genealogical Society, 1, 2, 3, 53
Spivey: Beth, **38**; Cainey, 37; Joe, 38; John "Furney", 38; Julia Ward, 14; Kitsey Bell Jacobs, 38; Norman, 38; Riley, 37
Spivey,: Albert Eddie, 14
St. Paul United Methodist Church, 39
Stanley: Molcey Stanley Cox, 38
Stephens: Cale, Capt., 34; Cora, *10*; F. Marion, 31; N. Boston, 48
Stevens: Rita Diane. *See* Jones, Rita Diane Stevens
Stone: Creasy Ivey, 12; Ellen. *See* Miller, Ellen Stone; Jacob, 12
Strawberries, **47**
Strawberry Festival, 52
Strole: Daniel F., 51; Glenn Franklin, 51; Inez Wilkes, 51; Jean Elizabeth. *See* Holland, Jean Elizabeth Strole; John Philip, 51; Rachel Estelle. *See* Matthews, Rachel Estelle Strole
Sunny South Colony, 47, 52
Superintendent of Public Instruction, 29
Sutton: Paul, 18
Tabor City, 35, 37, 38
Tabor City Crate Factory, 38
Tabor Primitive Baptist Church, 44
Tatum Township, 32
Tedder: Caroline, *16*; James D., *16*; Marshal, 16
Thomas: June, *10*; Will C., 31
Thompson: Harriet. *See* Hammond, Harriet Thompson; Lee. *See* Loman, Lee Thompson; Roland, 15; Sallie, 13
Thurman: Sonny Boy, 25
Todd: Belinda Beth. *See* White, Belinda Beth Todd; Lorenza, 35
Tooley: Lucy Ann. *See* Whitney, Lucy Ann Tooley

Toys, 45
Trask: Joseph H., 50; Louise I., 50; Nettie M., 50; Roy Edmund, 50; Samuel E., 50
Treadwell: Elizabeth. *See* Wooten, Elizabeth Treadwell; John, Major, 11; Mary. *See* Wooten, Mary Treadwell
Troy: Bernard, 6; John, 6
Tudor: John, 30
Tyler: Ruby Ethel. *See* Miller, Ruby Ethel Tyler
Usher: Bertha Howe, 49; William White, 49
Vinegar Hill, 44
Waddell: Willie, 7
Walker: Beryl Pifer Whitlow, 50; Betty Rose, 40; Dewey, **40**; Emily Manning, 40; Hilda Grey, 40; M. M., 48; William George, 40
Ward: Anzaline Harrelson, 44; Henry, 14; John William, 44; Julia. *See* Julia Ward Spivey; Kit, 38; Lillon. *See* Wright, Lillon Ward; Lina, 18; Poton, *16*
Watts: Ann Hinson, 39; Anna Eliza, 38; Eli Sr., 39; Eliza (Ressie). *See* Arp, Eliza (Ressie) Watts; Lou Floy. *See* Milligan, Lou Floy Watts; Mary, 35; Mary Ann, 39
Wayne: George, *28*; Inez, 15; Rhodes, 15, *16*, *17*
Wesley: Edward, 50; Frank, 50; Irene, 50; John Deming, 50; Joseph Patrick, 50; Josephine, 50; Louetta, 50; Mary, 50
West: Gladys, 18
Western Prong, 10
Weyman Creek, 5
White: "Peanut", *32*; Amma Gurganious, 13, *See* White, Amma Gurganious; Belinda Beth Todd, 13; Beverly Larue. *See* Lynn, Beverly Larue White; Charles, 50, 51; Clarie Amma. *See* McQueen, Clarie Amma White; Clarie Dexter, Jr., 13; Clarie Dexter, Sr., 13; Ferry Gertrude Smith, 14, John, 50, 51; Larry Dean, 13; Marion H.. *See* McWhorter, Marion H. White; Mary Sadler Miller, 13, *14*; Nancy Holcomb. *See* King, Nancy Holcomb White, *See* King, Nancy Holcomb White; Naomi Black, 13; Penny Kay. *See* Lynn, Penny Kay White; Phillip Charles, 13; Sandy Benjamin, 13; Tammy Sue, 13; Tressie Lorraine, 13
Whitener: Emma, 50; James E., 50; James S., 50; John I., 50
Whiteville, 3, 14
Whiteville-Conwayborough Road, 43
Whitlow: Beryl Pifer. *See* Walker, Beryl Pifer Andrews
Whitney: Cornelius, 50; Harvey, 50, 51; Lottie. *See* Covil, Lottie Whitney; Lucy Ann Tooley, 50
Wilkes: Inez. *See* Strole, Inez Wilkes
Williams: Elizabeth Jane. *See* Wooten, Elizabeth Jane; Grace Louise. *See* Harnly or Harnley, Grace Louise Williams; John E., 49
Williamson: Archie, 53; Clara Elizabeth Martin, 53; Lenworth. Earl "Earl", *53 - 58*; Gaston, 31; James, 51; Michael Stephen, 54
Wilmington Charlotte, and Rutherford Railroad, 5
Wilson: Alice, 50; Arthur, *20*; Bonnie, 20; Charles D., *20*; Charlie, 27; Christine, *20*; Dixie. *See* Rogers, Dixie Wilson; George Prosise, 15, 20, *20*; 27; Herman J., 50; John W., *20*; Kitty Prosise, *20*; Margaret Brown, **15 - 25**, *15*; Olivia Baldwin, 27
Wooten: Allen, 10, 11; Anne M., 12; Caroline Matilda, 11; Charity. *See* Grissette, Charity Wooten; Charlotte M., 12; Edgar, *10*; Edward Williams, 11; Eliza Jane, 11; Elizabeth, 11; Elizabeth Allen, 10; Elizabeth C., 12; Elizabeth Jane Williams, 11; Elizabeth Morphis, 11; Elvira Davis, 10; Frances M., 11; Frank T., Rev., 28; F. L., *29*; Helen, 11; Henrietta T., 12; Henry, *10*, 11; Herbert, Mrs, *10*; Ida McCallum, *10*; Jessie. *See* Council, Jessie Wooten; John, 10, 11; John A., 12; John Council, 11; John F., Col., 11; John Henry, 12; John William, 11; Josephine "Joanna", 11; Macon, Jr., 10; Mary (Duhadway) Singletary, 11; Mary Cromartie, 12; Mary Hodge, 11; Mary Potts, *10*; Mary Treadwell, 10; Narcissa Dorsey, 11; Rachel, 11; Richard, 10, 11; Richard L., Gen., 11; Richard Lafayette, 11; Robert, 10, 12; Robert Alexander, 11; Robert D., 11; Sallie Clark, *10*; Sara Eliza, 11; Sarah Elvira Davis, 12; Sarah Lucy Oliver, 11; Selina, 11; Shadrach, **10**; Shadrach, III, 12; Shadrach, IV, 12; Shadrach, Jr., 10, 11; Thomas Box, 10, 11; Thomas J., Major, 11; Thomas Jones, 11; William, 12; William Davis, 12
Wright: Balzura. *See* Porter, Balzura Wright; Hance, **38**; Hansen, 38; Kenyon, 38; Lawson "Loss", 37; Lennon, 39; Lillon Ward, **44**; Lucian Dow, 39; Maloy, 44; Mayon, 44; Oscar, 31; Prudence Norris, 38; Sarah Soles "Sis", 38; Simpson, 38; Sis Joyner, 38; Thomas I, 6; Williard, 39
Wright Cemetery, 38
Wyche: Bryan, 28, *29*; Bryon, *17*; Henry, 28; James A., *16*; Jim, *29*; Mary B., 28; Melba, 15
Yates: Catherine Simmons, 3, *52*; Lee. *See* McLean, Lee Yates; Martha, 53; Robert Allen, Dr., 52; Robert Allen, Jr., 52
Young: Mariah, *16*; Obadiah, *26*
Zigler: Mary E.. *See* Pifer, Mary E. Zigler

www.ingramcontent.com/pod-product-compliance
Ingram Content Group UK Ltd.
Pitfield, Milton Keynes, MK11 3LW, UK
UKHW051117200426
11947UKWH00038B/1886